Child Hunters

Child Hunters

Requiem of a Childkiller

CARINE HUTSEBAUT

Copyright © 2011 by Carine Hutsebaut.

Cover illustration: Gottfried Helnwein-Judaskiss

ISBN: Softcover   978-1-4653-0428-5
               Ebook   978-1-4653-0427-8

All rights reserved. No part of this book may be reproduced or transmitted in any form or by any means, electronic or mechanical, including photocopying, recording, or by any information storage and retrieval system, without permission in writing from the copyright owner.

This book was printed in the United States of America.

To order additional copies of this book, contact:
Xlibris Corporation
0-800-644-6988
www.XlibrisPublishing.co.uk
Orders@XlibrisPublishing.co.uk

Contents

PART I
The Paedosexual Crime

1. The Story of John (Part One) 11
2. The Paedosexual crime 23
3. Six Types of Paedosexual offenders 43
   - a) The sexual explosive and sadistic criminal 44
   - b) The Anger Rapist 45
   - c) The fixated Paedosexual 46
   - d) The Paedosexual in regression 49
   - e) The Sexual Rapist 53
   - f) The Social Rapist 54
4. The cycle in the Paedosexual Crime 57
5. Why victims don't talk 61

PART II
From Sexual Abuse to Child Murder

6. The Story of John (Part II) 73
7. Anger is a verb 97
8. The Role of Pornography in Childhood 105
9. Profiles of Child Killers 111

PART III
Case Studies

10. Janet 125
11. Emma 137
12. Victoria 143
13. Evelyn and Peter, Victims of a paedosexual crime? 149

PART IV
Pedosexuality and Society

14. John's Story (Part III) 173
15. Public Opinion and the Media 185
16. An International Approach 195

PART V
Therapy and Prevention

17. The Gracewell Institute of Birmingham 207
18. An Efficient Approach 217
19. Victimology 223
20. Prevention and Victim Aid 235

Conclusions 245
Appendices 251

In the Wrinkles of my Soul

In the wrinkles of my soul

I carefully saved tears

To calm the danger,

That sneakily threatens my heart.

Through the dark corridors,

Furtively sneak in those thoughts,

That fear for the light

When I convulsively

Vomit . . .

NO!!!!!

Eva Van den Eynde

PART I

The Paedosexual Crime

CHAPTER 1

The Story of John (Part One)

A quite child

The war is over and everyday life can begin again. Just as it does for our family Davies. living on the outskirts of Rotterdam. Taking the bad with the good they too would like to start over again. Gerrit and Lisa already have three children, two girls and a boy, when a new baby is born. They name the newborn John. In the first years of his life John does not have any significant problems. He grows up to be a quiet though slightly introvert toddler. Nevertheless you can often see him playing with children from the neighborhood and hanging around with his sisters and brother. There are plenty of things to do in the neighborhood: there are moorlands, forests, and creeks.

But John has these strange habits that no one can explain. When for instance he sees something very beautiful, he clenches his little fists and rubs them roughly against his eyes. Sometimes he hides them behind his back where he tries to restrain them while they're wriggling continuously. It looks as if he has got an uncontrollable urge to destroy such beauty, but the fear of getting slapped keeps him from doing so.

John's father is a violent man. He drinks excessively and then beats his wife. The children avoid him, because they too are not spared by the father when he has been drinking. When he is sober he shows himself to be a good father and a model husband. His drinking mates often come to the house, Lisa is not happy with that. She has enough on her plate taking care of the household chores and needs every penny to manage. A lot of money however is squandered in bars, Gerrit's drinking causes tensions in the family that lead to violent outbursts.

Lisa's sister, Mien, often helps the family out. She does so on her own terms. Although she does not have any children of her own she likes to think she knows better. She is very bossy; more than once she will act like she is the mother and do things her way. She is tough. Maaike, one of the children often collides with her. Maaike, it has to be said, is not easy-going. If she does not want to eat, like most days, aunt Mien will stuff the food into her mouth. Often there will be a fight, because Maaike won't let herself be overpowered by aunt Mien.

Removed from the nest

By the time John is two years old, another baby boy is born. Aunt Mien has had just about enough of it now. Helping out, with five children running about is just too much. She tries to persuade Lisa to give up one of her children. She goes on and on and finally she has her way. Mien wants the new baby, but somewhat later she reconsiders her decision: she prefers little John.

Mien promises Lisa that she will visit regularly with John and takes the little boy with her. He has just turned four years old and does not know what is happening to him. Up until then he has seen a lot of violence; his mother frequently ends up in the hospital, for reasons he does not understand, once he saw his father smashing his mother's head through the window. She ran into the street bleeding. That time she spent the night at the neighbor's house. In their opinion they don't think it will be a good idea for Lisa to press charges against her husband. "It can only harm your reputation," they said. Of course Lisa is too ashamed to talk about the humiliations she has to go through day after day.

Recently there is more going on, for a while now she feels like there is something wrong between her husband and her daughter Maaike, but she feels too helpless to bring the subject up. Later on it turns out that her husband had been raping Maaike since she was three years old. John slept in that same room. He must have witnessed this every time.

Maaike has been impossible to handle since she was a toddler and her behavior becomes more and more unpredictable. She is arrogant, disobedient and acts savagely. She burns her arms with cigarettes, frequently she uses sharp objects to cut them severely, then runs to her mother a few moments later laughing hysterically showing her bleeding arms. Many years later Maaike will tell me her mother underwent several abortions because her father did not want any more children. They performed the abortions at home. Once in a while things went wrong and there would be an ambulance at the front of the door. At least eight times, according to Maaike, her mother was taken away in those circumstances. Mother Lisa is so afraid of her husband she does not tell a soul about what is going on.

John has been living with his aunt Mien for a couple of weeks now, when she calmly announces she is moving to Paris, of course she is taking little John with her. Her husband had found himself a good job there and the child would have a better upbringing. Lisa was overwhelmed. Of course aunt Mien promises her sister that she will take good care of her little boy and visit her many times.

An ever growing isolation

Paris: yet again a radical change. John is not familiar with the language, yet French is the only language used in his new home. John who is very shy, feels like everything is slipping away from him and often his thoughts are in the Netherlands (with his family). He compensates his powerlessness with violent fantasies in which he takes revenge for personal afflicted harm. In Paris John has no friends. Not only is there a language barrier, but also on top of that he is not allowed to play in the streets with other children. He has no chance of exploring nature, in Paris there are no woods and fields and the little Parisian parks are off limits to him. His 'new mama' reduces him to being a precious porcelain doll which stands quietly on the mantelpiece.

John's uncle is a weak person, not for one moment does he think of challenging his wife's decisions. Mind you he does not even want to interfere in bringing up John, who is just a toy for his wife. The caring of children is women's domain, that is his motto. John's uncle is not home very often and John does not remember him that much.

John is not short of material things but when it comes to the emotional and social development the little boy is severely deprived and ultimately harmed. Almost every branch of the growing tree is being cut off. He is growing up to be a shapeless, vulnerable conifer. The timid child has to join the tea-parties of aunt Mien. Posh ladies taking a sips from their cup of tea, little pinkies in the air, little dish in the left hand. They chatter enjoyably and catch up on the latest gossip. Nose pressed against the window John looks with sad despairing eyes out into the world. From that moment on window glass will represent the invisible border between himself and reality.

Deep within himself he hates those women with all the power inside of him. Them and all other people. Behind his unseeing eyes there is a screen that shows scenes that no one has any idea of. On that screen he sees all those babbling women as slaves, his slaves. To his own heart's content he can rule over them, with one snap of his fingers they will obey him. He can make them dance to his tune. They are even prepared to die if that is what he wants. He reigns mercilessly and his authority is unquestionable.

Thinking about his mother, his brothers and sisters, John is feeling very homesick. The boy cannot understand how they seem to have forgotten him. He writes to them, but nobody ever writes back. Not until (only) forty years later John hears about the many letters his sister Maaike wrote to him. She misses her brother very much and feels sorry for him having to live with aunt Mien. John does not get to see a single letter from his sister.

When aunt Mien catches little John crying, she shows no sympathy whatsoever. Abruptly she commands him to stop, boys do not cry. On top of that she slanders the image of his mother. John has to hear just how bad a mother she is. For months he is exposed to tirades about his mother, one after the other. In the end he is afraid to even mention his mother and every night he muffles the sound of his crying in bed, and so, one by one his roots are cut off.

Once a year they would go to Rotterdam. While his brothers and sisters are playing in the streets he can only watch, standing next to his 'new mama'. He is not allowed to mess up his polished shoes and Parisian suit, otherwise he will be in trouble. Aunt Mien would get very angry and he knows her outbursts all too well. He knows she is a hard hitter when something is not to her liking. She always does that, even when he is not to blame.

Everything gets tangled up for John. He has trouble figuring out the family relations. In Paris, for instance, he has to address anybody with two legs as 'aunt' or 'uncle'. But John does not know anything about aunt Mien and her husband's circle of friends. Aunt Jolien, Uncle Kees, Aunt Tinny, Aunt Jo and so on. But are they really aunts and uncles? John soon finds out it really does not matter whether you like someone or not. That does not matter. What matters is: to see and to be seen.

Slavish and obedient like a puppy John walks along in this fancy, posh world. He sits up straight and hands out like paws when asked; people love him for it, but they are just joking. And when he is told: 'down boy', John disappears from their sight.

One severe blow after the other

But there is more than just tea-parties. Every week a distinguished gentlemen comes to pick John up in an expensive Cadillac with a driver. John is terrified of that man. Just to hear his name, even after forty years, is enough to send shivers up and down his spine. Mr Duchateau, that is his name, however brings him candy each time. Aunt Mien thinks he is so nice and refined, and John has to go with him, even though he has not got any children of his own with who John could play with. What does this man do with John? What kind of games does he make up? What is it that terrifies John so much, the days before he will be picked up his stomach aches? Why are John's knees shaking when hearing the low dark voice in the hallway? Who is that man and why does he pick up a seven-year-old boy every week?

He does not belong to the 'family', neither is he part of his aunt's circle of friends. For many years he played a significant role in John's life. When the time comes for John to find a job, he will work for Mr Duchateau.

John remembers being troubled by nightmares since he was five years old. At the age of seven he tries to commit suicide for the first time. He hits himself over the head with a bronze statue. He wants to die. Even at that age he struggles with extremely violent fantasies. Torture being the leading topic. Lisa told me her son was already seeing a psychiatrist at the age of twelve. She never got any explanation from her sister as to why he had to be treated. On top of that he was given heavy medication for such a small boy.

By the time he is twelve years old, John has to deal with serious identification problems: One time he is a female fairy tale character, and another time he is a man.

John is having some problems with Latin, his aunt and uncle decide he needs some coaching. This is strongly advised by the 'professor'. Coaching has already helped many other children. For a period of six months John is being raped every week by that teacher. If he performs well during the lessons he gets to suck the teacher's penis, if he is inattentive he will be sodomized (raped). To John it does not matter if he performs well or not. No matter how, John is being punished.

Confusion grows for the child. He cannot talk to any one about this. He is so ashamed it does not even occur to him to tell anybody. He thinks his aunt and uncle know about this and have even asked the teacher to do these things. In his eyes they control every aspect of his life. They determine what he thinks and what he does. He has no doubt his aunt and uncle are responsible for what happens to him during coaching. After all they pay the 'professor'.

John is not the only victim. Another boy starts to talk, a discreet investigation shows that several boys had gone through the same thing.

John too has to tell his story about the sexual violence. Aunt Mien is unmoved and does not talk to him for several days. Later on she tries to convince John that none of it is real and he just dreamt it. At any cost she wants to deny this horrible reality, demanding John to do the same, because of that he actually starts to doubt himself after a while. With his suppressed maturity he questions everything. Is this real or I am dreaming? Did I really see all that or was it my imagination? Did I really experience this or is it, like Aunt Mien says, a figment of my imagination.

Desperately John is looking for an end to this terrifying labyrinth. He does so by expanding his parallel universe. There he can express his fears and insecurities, his isolation and hatred, his powerlessness and confusion. In that world everything is perfectly clear. He rules over it; as long as he dictates what needs to be done, nothing can go wrong. There he finds peace. Every time something tends to go wrong in reality, he withdraws into himself. In his fantasy world he knows what to do with things that bother him.

In that same period of time another change messes up his life again. One day aunt Mien asks him how he would feel if she were to 'give' him a little sister. She has a four year old orphan girl in mind. It is almost like asking him if he wants a new bike. Of course he wants a brand-new bike. Who would say no to that? The ready-made in Italy bought, child takes up a lot of space. John has to give up more and more room. The pre-adolescent is considered to be more and more of a hassle, something that only disturbs mother's new-found bliss. Aunt Mien decides to get rid of him and sends him to boarding school, far away from Paris.

Boarding school is hell for John. He has never been without aunt Mien before. He feels lost in a place where the other boys soon find out he is weak. They often tease him and make him run the gauntlet. He is no match for their harassments. He had never learned to defend himself. At night John feels crushed by this harsh world and cries himself to sleep.

Every two weeks he is allowed to go home. Only to find the 'new sister' is demanding all the love and attention from his aunt. Aunt Mien has got herself a new toy. John is no longer of any use. There is no room in the family for him anymore.

Parallel universes (worlds)

John is fourteen years old. He plays paedosexual games with his new sister and soon finds he can easily dominate her. He can even force her not to tell anybody about the things they do. She is his first real slave. If I talk about this now with John he is convinced Aunt Mien had suspected something. One time she catches him masturbating and loses control, she beats him, throws a crystal ashtray at his head, hurls reproaches at him and threatens him. At that moment in time he has already reached the stage where he masturbates compulsively. He masturbates ten times a day. It is the only way he can release the build-up tension. Masturbating gives him mixed feelings: on the one hand he feels guilty, on the other he is relieved. These feelings are manifested at the same time and that causes tension and conflict again. The tension keeps building up like that, leaving him no other option than to masturbate once again. That is how this kind of behavior becomes compulsive. This perverse circle will dominate him for the rest of his life.

For most of the time John is living in his own world. Motionless and silently staring into space, he has the most incredible adventures, which can only be described as *sex-explorations* (jargon?!). Everything starts to focus on sex. Sex is what relaxes him the most and what dominates his fantasies. Every situation he connects to sex in a perverted way. Nobody has any idea what goes on in his mind. It is his world and nobody from the cruel outside world is allowed in. It is his own private heaven where he has the divine and absolute power to decide who gets to live or die.

The way other boys fantasize about knights, jousts, castles and young ladies, John fantasizes about the most horrific things.

He does not care if people around him think these shocking stories are reprehensible. He does not belong to their world anyway. Nobody ever invited him to be part of it. John is finding it more and more difficult to differentiate between the two worlds. Real life and fantasy start to mix. This total isolation is too much to bear for this growing boy.

Rejected

John is four years old when he feels rejected for the first time: he feels as if his mother has abandoned him. When the new sister comes into the picture and aunt Mien gets rid of him after making him completely depend on her, he experiences a second rejection.

John is nineteen years old and stays in Germany for his teaching practice. He meets a girl. Despite being shy he finds the courage to ask her for a date in the park. He dresses up for her, buys her flowers and shows up way too early. He waits and waits. He waits for hours. It is starting to rain. She will come. She has to come. After a while it rains even harder. At dusk he looks for her in the park but she is nowhere to be found. The flowers are drooping and his hands are numb with cold but John is oblivious. The rain is pouring down when finally he decides to head back, soaking wet and sad.

John is twenty-one years old when he falls head over heels in love. Minouche is a fellow student at university. She is everything he has ever dreamt of. He succeeds in having a relationship with her. Because they skipped so many classes together they are forced to give up their studies. They spend their days having sex. The girl does everything for him. It does not even occur to John that this relationship might end one day. Things are not going well with them. John is so possessive, jealous and demanding, Minouche is becoming afraid of him. She asks for a few weeks respite so she can thinks things over. She goes away on a holiday. The day she is to return he arrives at the platform several hours too early and burning with desire. He has bought her flowers. His roses will stun her and make her melt. When the train enters the station John is bursting with impatience. A crowd of people make their way towards the exit, where John is waiting to meet her. She cannot miss him. He sees her, she laughs. His heart skips a beat. He wants to run to her but then he notices the smile was not meant for him. She did not even see John. Beside her walks a tall, lanky man who looks just as happy as she is. Jan is upset. He cannot stop staring at their joined hands. Cheerfully they pass him without even noticing he is there. Completely dazed and robot-like he heads towards the edge of the platform. He throws his flowers onto the tracks, sees a train approaching and jumps. A heart-rending cry freezes up the passengers. The train manages to come to a stop just in front of him. The driver is furious and shouts at John as he crawls back on the platform. I cannot even kill myself, he thinks, as he leaves with his tail between his legs. For five years John mourns over the loss of his Minouche.

Desperate and clumsy attempts

Meanwhile he has found a job as representative of a chain of supermarkets. John wants to do his best to succeed in life. He will do anything to please his boss. Nevertheless he is afraid of that man. One day he is invited to join him for breakfast. John would rather not accept the invitation, but reluctantly agrees. That morning he is welcomed by his boss and his wife, who is still in her nightgown. During breakfast many things are insinuated by the couple. John does not really understand what is implied. Then his boss makes it perfectly clear for him: he demands that John has sex with his wife while he is watching them. John retches. They are flabby fat people, he thinks they are absolutely gross.

Eventually he gives in to the threats of his boss. After all he could lose his job, and he can imagine how aunt Mien would react to that.

When John leaves the apartment in the morning he has to throw up. Blindly he drives the company car through heavy traffic. When he sees a truck heading towards him, he quickly turns the steering wheel and drives head-on into it. Miraculously he survives, but he has to stay in the hospital for several weeks. There he slips into a deep latent depression. When he returns to work John gets fired. His fears grow by the minute: fear of aunt Mien, fear of his boss, fear of himself, fear of what is to come, fear of life. A few months later he goes to the south of France with his uncle and aunt, which they do every year. They stay in a fancy holiday resort where a lot of rich Dutch people spend their holiday. John is a fairly attractive man. He spends his days alone; only a dog accompanies him. In a outdoor café he enjoys his soda. Out of the corner of his eye he sees some young people who are having fun. He would very much like to be part of them, but how does one make contact? How do you do that? Which girl should he talk to? He is afraid to take a chance out of fear of being laughed at. Imagine the girl telling him to take a hike. Without him noticing, a young blond girl comes over to him, her name is Anne and she asks him to join the gang. As if hypnotized John follows her. Feeling shy he sits down in the sand with the rest of the group. He enjoys hanging out with them. It is turning out to be a wonderful holiday. Although he is not really part of the gang, he is feeling less lonely.

One night the cheerful gang decide to go to the discotheque. John is asked to join them. He really wants to be the centre of attention and thinks of something to surprise the gang. With great concentration John stares at a wall, long enough for one of the lads to notice him.

'What's up John?'

'Don't you see the big purple butterflies on the wall?'

No one sees them.

'Well, look up there, on that white wall, hundreds of fluttering purple butterflies! Don't you see them? Where would they come from?'

The more John points to the butterflies, the less the others understand. Sweating, he gasps for breath. Finally he has got all the attention he so desperately wants. But nobody sees the spectacle of his hallucinating imagination. In the end he is escorted outside, so he can calm down a bit. What a spectacle! And everybody is concerned. For him! For that insignificant boy who never got any attention from anybody.

Under the guise (pretext) of normal life

John builds up a relationship with Anne. Meanwhile he continues to abuse his foster sister. A couple of months later the couple marry in full vestments. Anybody who wants to be noticed is present at the castle of Versailles. There are no friends of John's there because he has not got any. All the more important business relations and colleagues of his uncle walk around.

The couple have two children, a boy and a girl. Everything seems to be fine. Nobody knows that John frequently goes out looking for children. He brings them to his house when his wife is out. He ties them down on the bed and abuses them in a most perverse way. The need to dominate grows stronger and stronger. Because he cannot have his way with adult people he focuses on children. John acts like a model husband and good father, a jovial host and sociable colleague, but Anne has had the feeling for some time now that something is wrong with their marriage. She may be a naive young girl, straight out of boarding school, but that does not prevent her from realizing their sex life is not normal, and the problems do not fade away with the passing of the years.

One day John gets caught and has to go to prison for eighteen months on the charges of paedosexual acts with children from the neighborhood.

Anne has wanted to leave him for some time now. She has not any idea how to help him and the subject is not up for discussion. Every time he asked her to dress up like a child, she refused. She has her hands full protecting the children from him. John suggests shipping over a Pilipino girl to fulfill his needs. Anne also objects to that idea.

She is alone with this. She has got no one to confide in. It is after all a delicate subject. During his stay in prison Anne makes up a lot of excuses to conceal the truth. A divorce seems to be the best thing, but aunt Mien and her husband talk her out of that. After six months Anne goes to visit John in prison. When John gets out of prison he is without a job. Meanwhile Anne has found herself a job. Their little daughter does not know what is wrong with her daddy. She was told he was very sick and that he had to stay in the hospital for a long time. Their twelve year old son does know the truth.

CHAPTER 2

The Paedosexual crime

Definitions

In the common language terms as paedophilia and paedosexuality are usually mixed up. I want to make a clear distinction: Paedophilia can be considered as a disposition, Paedosexuality clearly means: sexual activity between an adult and a child. Not every paedophile is a paedosexual and very few paedosexuals are paedophiles. paedophilia comes from the word 'loving children'. In fact, caring parents could be considered as paedophiles. They would never do anything to harm their children or the integrity of their children.

Many paedophiles struggle a lifetime fight with themselves to 'keep their hands to themselves'.

Paedosexual handlings are punishable. It is a crime. In every kind of society all over the world, sexual activity between an adult and a child is morally reprehensible and legally punishable. Anthropological research in

New Guinea and Central America showed that primitive communities reject firmly any sexual activity between an adult and a child. The myth states that in Greece and Egypt, adults introduced children into the sexual world. This may be considered as paedosexual talk. There were incestuous relationships, but very often it was a matter of goods and power to be kept in the family.

Paedosexual abuse does not only mean rape. The term is much wider. Paedosexual abuse can be subtle, but therefore no less traumatic for a child. Subtle sexual abuse can be: a child that is forced to show her/his naked body, can be photographed for pornography, a child can be forced to watch sexual activity between two adults or forced to watch pornographic films. Less subtle forms of sexual abuse are: forced oral, vaginal or anal penetration; touching erogenous zones of an adult or another child, being touched by an adult. And yes, even sexual torture.

The definition of paedosexual abuse is: 'introducing a depending, immature child to sexual activities that it cannot understand or consent in.' Even if there should be 'consent' of a child, the activity still remains punishable. It is a crime.

Incest

Incest is a specific form of paedosexual abuse.

Mary is eighteen months old when she's sexually abused for the first time. She cannot exactly remember and is unable to find the right words to explain. As a baby she systematically refuses food and she loses a lot of weight. Every object that approaches her mouth makes her scream hysterically. She tightens her little lips. In her playpen she knocks her little head against the wooden rails for hours. Her mother decides to wrap her head in thick towels to protect it. Only fifty years later, she hears why her child was difficult as a baby. She never saw her husband abuse the child.

Mary is three years old when she runs away from home at least twice a week. Raising this child is a real torment, bedwetting, nightmares, epileptic crises, hysterical laughter. This child is uncontrollable. But Mary remembers precisely this: she's four years old and every night her father comes into her bedroom and rapes her. Sometimes he brings some of his friends with him. They can all have their part in the game. It all started when Mary was very little and therefore she cannot always find the right words to define what they did. She cannot speak properly under the age of four. She has no vocabulary to say the words that could explain what she endures. It will be a secret forever what happened in these early years, but there is no doubt: Mary was a victim of extreme sexual violence during her early childhood.

Mary is five years old. She stands on top of the stairway and stares into the depths, before her mother can intervene she throws herself down the stairs screaming hysterically Her laugh is frightening. The underlying scream for help is not understood by anybody.

Mary decides to seek help from God. God will help her because her teacher at school often talks about the almighty goodness of God. God loves children. Mary dreams away at her school desk and fantasizes about how God will take her in his protecting arms. Her thoughts are always miles away and the teacher cannot handle her anymore. Almost every day she sends Mary out into the corridor. When the teacher screams at her in class, Mary comes out from her desk, spreads her little legs and pees on the floor yelling loudly. Nobody understands this signal.

Mary has no escape from this torture, no time to rest. Every night her father comes. Nobody cares. She is seven years old when she finds the courage to see the priest of her community. She tells him what has been going on at home for so many years. All her hope is directed on him, but the priest becomes very, very angry. How can she say something as horrible as that about her father? How dare she invent such an incredible story. God will never allow her into heaven! Thou shalt honour thy father and thy mother! "Get out! You devil's child! Out of my church!" he yells at the little girl "Never dare to come back here and never dare to say such horrible things about your parents again!"

How can Mary come under God's eyes again? Only God can let her into his heaven and now, by the words of the priest, he has closed that door forever.

Sadly she returns home. Mary remembers that it rained that day, another sad day in her young life. Her beautiful dreams explode. She decides to not listen to all these 'God-stories' anymore and she also decides to not go home anymore. She wanders through the streets of Eindhoven and falls asleep, exhausted, hours later in a deserted porch. It is cold and there are a lot of soldiers in the streets because there is a war (world war II). Two soldiers find this girl sleeping and cold. It is late at night when they deliver the little girl to her father. The following days, Mary is even more unmanageable. She is terrified because she had talked about the 'secret' with somebody. Her father had warned her: if she ever talked about what happened he would kill every person Mary loves, one by one. Hopefully nothing will happen to grandma, Mary thinks while she looks through the classroom window. The only place where she is safe is with grandma. On her lap she can dream away and daddy cannot hurt her. Grandma often plays with Mary in the orchard. She can eat the ripe apples and put them in the basket. She has the loveliest grandma in the world.

Some days later, grandma dies. The grief of the little girl is endless. Even greater is her fear of her father. Obviously he is able to make the people she loves, die.

At school the head teacher calls a meeting. The problem with this child cannot continue. They advise the parents to take her to a psychiatrist. Three psychiatrists examine the girl. Mary knows the risks of talking. She can only explain via drawings that her world is extremely painful. The drawings are so horrific in form and content that the psychiatrists decide to take the child to a mental hospital. Nobody seems to understand what is wrong with her. It is 1944. The war is still on. Sexual abuse is a taboo subject. The doctors decide that the child is a typical case of 'Female hysteria'. They'll 'fix' her. Every day they submit the hysterical little girl to electric shock treatment. When Mary is not on the pain table, she's in an isolation cell, bound at her feet and wrists. Nine days she will stay isolated on that bed. Apart from the people that come to feed her, she sees nobody. Mary is a fighter, but every time she tries to resist with the little strength that is left, she is punished with an ice cold bath for hours. The doctors want to break the strong will of that bewildered child.

Father comes to get her. He probably becomes scared that she might finally start to talk. Or maybe he needs her again to reduce his own frustrations? Or maybe he gets money from his friends in exchange for the rapes of his little girl? Maybe he needs that money? It is too long ago to find this out. The hell goes on. Because of the years of rape, Mary is not menstruating normally. She's sixteen when she has her period for the first time. She remembers being pregnant eight times. Every time she was bound on the kitchen table while her father and his friends took care of the 'evidence' in and around her body. She even remembers she had to go and bury a fetus of seven months in the back garden.

Mary runs away from home when she is pregnant for the ninth time. She is eighteen, a minor at that time. She never set foot into that house of horrors again. Nonetheless she is the only one of all the children that visits her father after many years. Her father is dying from liver cancer, the result of years of alcohol abuse. Every day she tries to ease the pain. Does she hope for a word of regret? Does she hope that he will ask her to forgive him before he dies? Does she hope to know why he did all those things to her? Her father owes her these answers forever. He died thirty years ago. Mary is still looking for the answer to her 'why?' She survives, but a real life is impossible for her. She still suffers from extremely severe asthma crises, auto mutilations and epileptically convulsions. She has been in treatment for over thirty years. She cannot be repaired. Her doctor, a specialist in extreme long-term sexual violence, told me that it is a miracle she's still alive. He compiled a document for me for a later trial in the case of her brother.

Her family denies the facts, but Mary was courageous and told me her whole story. Her brother suppressed his traumas, with all the consequences one can imagine. He murdered two little girls and will never be released from prison. He slept in the same room as his sister. He witnessed all the sexual violence for years. He was too small to do anything and it is very obvious that the connection between sexual violence, frustration and sexual excitement marked him for the rest of his life.

We have to urgently take our responsibilities and recognize the signals sexual abused children send out. The initiative and the approach of a potential victim have to come from us. We cannot expect this from a traumatized, often threatened victim. The victim has already too many barriers and fears to fight, to stay alive. We don't have these obstacles. The question: "how are you?" is to less posed.

With incest victims we often see a double attitude towards the offender.

A child does not easily bear a grudge towards an adult. It reacts totally different from an adult. A child does not see the things in the larger context as we do, but more as separate items and facts. We can hear a child say: "Now I love my daddy because he bought me a nice bicycle," and later the same child says: "I hate my daddy because he touched my wee wee." Or, "sometimes I don't like my older brother because he does things to me that I don't like and that confuses me." An adult would more easily reject the other in general because of a minor disagreement.

A child is overwhelmingly generous and forgiving and that is exactly what the offender takes advantage of. Many therapists and psychiatrists do not understand these double standards of children. Too often they decide that the child must have invented the incest story, by doing so they avoid a confrontation with the criminal. Many professionals do not know how to talk about such a serious subject as child sexual abuse. They feel it is embarrassing and often cannot find the words themselves to talk about it with the victim. They should find themselves another job or find a good therapist for themselves first.

Many children do not want their daddy to go to jail. They only want him to not do these things anymore. Especially young children need their father and are prepared to make tremendous sacrifices to keep him. Even admitting they lied, when they didn't. The child does not want to feel guilt for the fact that his talking led his father right into prison. This item must be treated with great respect for what the child wants and what is best to protect the child from further abuse. A good point would be to involve the victim in the process of punishment for the offender, especially if this is his/her father. Past experiences have shown us that a prison sentence on its own is not effective. It is necessary that the offender be compelled to undergo specialized treatment with, for this purpose, specially trained professionals. (See further: the criteria for working with child sex offenders).

We often see that the obliged treatment for the offender has a healing effect on the victim as well, especially when the victim is informed about the progress or the eventual relapses of the offender. On the other hand, it is also absolutely necessary that the offender go to prison, even if it is only for some months. This makes immediate clear to the victim that she or he is not guilty of the abuse, but the offender. Everybody knows that the criminal is punished and not the victim. Although child sex offenders very often think they are the victims, or they behave as if they are the victims in the whole process. Many of them accuse the victim: "She seduced me . . . She wanted this . . . I saw her looking at my genitals . . . I only taught her about sex! I'm not a Dutroux, I was always careful . . . I didn't force her . . . I did not hurt her or him . . ."

It is already half of the treatment program for a victim when the abuser is sentenced to prison by a judge, because most of the time, the largest problem for the victim is the feeling of guilt. "I must have provoked it." Or "I must be bad." Or "Why didn't I say 'no'? Boys sometimes feel more frustrated than girls. When they are older, they forget how it was to be an innocent little boy. They think with their big bodies that they should have fought the offender. "I should have hit him in the balls" said Edward to me while his face became all red with anger. "I should have taken a knife and planted it between his ribs!" Edward forgot that there was nothing he could have done. He's sixteen now, but he was only four when a neighbor raped him.

The Justice Department has an important role to play and it is seen in our Western Society that these departments often forget what exactly their real role is. In fact it is simple: it represents the whole society to judge what goes wrong. And what does society want?

It wants:

1. Punishment for the crime
2. Reparation if possible
3. Avoid relaps.

Our Justice Departments is so used to working with the criminals that she forgets all about the victims. Victims hardly have a role in the whole picture. It is important for victims that the Justice Departments treat their cases well because they represent a whole society. It is all right that mum and dad and the whole family believe the victim, but it is not enough, the Justice Department has to believe the victim too. Only then can a victim start working her/his way out of the victim status and become healed from the traumas. There must be no doubt left.

Denial

For centuries the awful truth about sexual violence has been denied.
Worse: the victims themselves were responsible for the crime. Although research since the 1920s has consistently documented a high prevalence of sexual abuse, the information has been largely ignored by professionals and seldom made available to the public (Salter, 1988). A convenient theory was used to explain the numbers of adult women complaining of sexual abuse as children. They were victims, not of sex offenders, but of Oedipal fantasies (Masson 1984). Those adults and children who were acknowledged to have been abused frequently found themselves blamed for the attacks. Abraham wrote in 1972 that:

"... Female hysterics in particular are constantly meeting with adventures. They are molested in the public street; outrageous sexual assaults are made on them etc ... It is part of their nature that they must expose themselves to external traumatic influences. There is in them a need to appear to be constantly subjected to external violence. In this we recognize a general psychological characteristic of women in an exaggerated form ...."

Anne Salter continues:

"... Throughout this century young child victims have been frequently described as 'seductive' or 'provocative' (Mohr, Turner, Jerry 1964, Revitch & Weiss, 1962 ; Virkkunen, 1975). The clinical bases for these observations were sometimes interviews with the offender alone. Revitch and Weiss (1962) noted that, 'we rarely had the opportunity of examining the victims of paedophiles; however, we had the clinical impression that quite often the child victim is aggressive and seductive and often induces the adult offender to commit the offence'. In a 1981 article Virkkunen implied the offender's word should be taken over the official records in a study in which the two differed as to the degree of 'victim participation'. Under such circumstances there could be little interest in treating sex offenders. Some authors, in fact, suggested that it was the 'participating victims' who were in need of treatment. 'Unlike most other sex crimes the male offender in cases of statutory rape has no special pathology; the girl is usually more in need of psychiatric care or other attention'. (Slovenko, 1971) ...."

I have, and still am working with child sex offenders and victims of sexual abuse for over twenty years. It always amazed me that 'professionals' can understand a sex offender, without ever having seen a victim and the opposite picture. How can one understand a victim without knowing how a sex offender thinks? Maybe these professionals are just smarter than I am, but believe me I would not be able to understand either of them without seeing both.

I'll give an example:

Mister Morgan, notoir sex offender, claims in his treatment:

"But, Miss Hutsebaut, I assure you that Sharon was laughing. She liked it."

Who am I to doubt this? Why would he lie about such a detail? I decided to ask the victim:

"Sharon, I know it is difficult, but can you explain to me what you did while Mister Morgan was abusing you?"

Sharon begins to turn on her chair. She dares not look at me. She fixes her gaze on the wall behind my back.

"Well, you know, I didn't know what to do. I felt so embarrassed. I felt so ashamed. He was so big and I was so small. I was so confused, you know"

Me: "I can imagine. But please, tell me what exactly did you do?"

Sharon: "I laughed. I felt so confused and ashamed."

Me: "So you laughed because you didn't know what to do?"

Sharon: "Yes." She looks to the ground.

Now, if we analyze the situation, we can state that Mister Morgan did not lie. Indeed, Sharon laughed. But . . . in fact the trap is here: Mister Morgan's observations are right. She laughed. But his interpretations are wrong. She did not laugh because she liked it. She laughed because she was embarrassed.

Another example:

Mister Becker:

"She was a little woman, as seductive as an adult. She sat on top of the back rest in my car. I could see her little white slip in my mirror."

Me: "How old was Betty?"

He: "She was five, but I assure you she was provoking me."

Now, tell me which girl takes notice of her underpants at that age!
It is almost unbelievable that adult professionals take this rubbish for truth. But they did and they harmed thousands of victims for more then a

century. And nobody did anything to oppose such statements. People like Anne Salter and many others, finally did. And little by little things change.

That is why it is my opinion that all these professionals mentioned above are as incompetent as possibly can be. They take the statement of professional liars for granted and they decide to not believe a victim or even examine any discrepancies in the statements there might be. How 'professional' can one be? Some people laugh at funerals not because they are happy to be at a funeral or because they are happy with someone's death, but because they feel nervous.

Journalists often ask me in television programs and for newspapers which do I think is the most dangerous serial killer in the world. I always start with the one at the top of my list: Sigmund Freud, followed by Abraham, Masson and a lot of those other 'so-called' specialists. I wonder what really went on in these men's minds. They are responsible for centuries-long denial of what is the most horrible crime in human life. They are the accomplices of the criminals themselves for they covered their crimes. The most dramatic of all this is that their theories and 'so-called' trustworthy studies are still taught at universities all over the world!

Figures

More than fifteen years ago, I began to realize that the situation of child sex abuse started to take a dramatic form. This is not amazing because specialists all over the world claim that a Paedosexual can have abused 200 victims during his sexual active life. Ernie Allen of the NCMEC (National Centre for Missing and Exploited Children, USA) speaks of 120. In one of the best books in the world about that subject: Working with sex offenders (Michael A. O'Connell, Eric Leberg and Craig R. Donaldson) Anna C. Salter, a world specialist in the field, states:

> ". . . Reliable research finds the prevalence of child sexual abuse of females to be from 28 to 38 % of the population, depending on whether you study girls under 14 or under 18 (Russell, 1984) Almost

half (44 %) of the adult women in Russell's methodologically sound study had been the victims of either rape or attempted rape . . . ."

"With the admission of the prevalence of sexual abuse and the beginning of widespread sex offender treatment programs, the chronicity and repetitiveness of sexual aggression without treatment has begun to be recognized. Abel et al. (1987) found that the average female-oriented paedophile had 20 victims and the average male-oriented paedophile 150. In their voluntary and confidential study, 232 child molesters admitted to having over 17.000 victims under the age of 14. When all types of paraphiliac acts were included 561 sex offenders admitted to over 291.000 deviant acts with a total of over 195.000 victims . . . ."

Scary figures.

The specialized Gracewell Institute of Birmingham speaks about the fact that 25 % of the abused boys become child sex offenders when they are adults. Together they will make again hundreds of new victims. This means that, in two generations, we start from one offender and end up with thousands of victims. The French Ministry of Health admitted that 25 % of the children are victims of sexual abuse.

The offenders

Sexual abuse of children happens in all levels of society. Almost 80 % of the abuse happens within the family.

When we hear the word Paedosexual we spontaneously think of men. Do women abuse children sexually too? Do women kill children in a sexual context too? There have not been any profound studies yet. But specialists in the field presume that 4 % of the child sex offenders are women. This figure is increasing rapidly. Until some years ago a female victim accused herself of the abuse. It was part of the hypocrite religious education that girls or women were responsible for the behavior of men. Even in the 80's and the 90's the idea was that a girl or woman who was raped, was guilty of that crime. What was she doing alone in that street at that late hour? Have you seen how she was dressed?

It is strange to realize that when we call the authorities to report a burglary that these kinds of questions never occur. I have never heard a police officer ask such a victim: "Why were you not at home at the time of the burglary? What were you doing at that time? Can you prove that? How were you dressed? Can you prove that you have been robbed? . . ."

A heavy taboo is resting on female child sex offenders. Everybody expects a mother to cuddle a child and to caress it with love and attention. And yes, we sometimes hear that mothers sleep with their sons, but what does this represent? I never thought of a sexual connotation. So, for me too it was a taboo until some years ago. I heard victims telling me how women had raped them with all kind of objects, sometimes in groups with men. Women appear to be more cruel than men during sex 'parties'. A little boy of seven told me that he had been abused for several years by two female teachers at school. They took selected children to the basement of the school where other male offenders waited for a 'sex party' with children. The little boy told me that binding elastic around his little penis excited one of the female teachers. When the organ was swollen and almost blue, she took the elastic with two fingers, pulled it back and released it again. The pain for the little boy was unbearable. Men torture too, but not in such a sophisticated way. Men are more brutal while women use more fantasy.

Women in therapy admitted also to having forced young children to oral sex. At first they wanted me to believe they only did that to 'initiate' children into the sexual world. What difference is there between that excuse coming from women or from men? There is none. Both do it for their own sexual pleasure. We almost never read about women torturing their own or other children sexually. The taboo is too big. But it happens.

In the Netherlands there is the story of Yolanda of Epe (little town). A few years ago she wrote a book about her agony as a young girl. The whole story is in one word: gruesome. At the base of the physical and sexual abuse was her mother. In her book Yolanda describes how her mother got an orgasm while she was telling the story of the sexual torture of her daughter, while the police questioned her. Neighbors, people of the town, friends, policemen and even priests were clients on the scale of rapists at the house of Yolanda. Her mother was present in all the inhuman scenes and even encouraged her accomplices in their perversities. Yolanda has endured these tortures for years and many professionals wonder how this child survived this emotionally and morally. There must be a strong child hidden there, a child that . . . despite everything . . . wants to live. She did. Yolanda is marked for the rest of her life that is for sure. Luckily this kind of crime is exceptional, but it happens more then we suspect.

After this trial in the Netherlands, another young woman started to talk. She too has been the victim of extreme serious child maltreatment during her childhood.

Kelly

In Belgium I know of a case of a 40-year-old woman, Kelly. She has been raped by highly placed people in our society with the knowledge of her parents. They were paid to 'lease' their children.

When Kelly, three years old, and her little sister were put to bed, there was no question of relaxation and rest. They lay there asking themselves if their parents would come up again to wake them and carry them to a fancy car waiting at the front door. They never knew to where they were taken. But what they had to endure was indescribable.

"There have been moments that I pretended to sleep, hoping that my parents would take my sister lying next to me in bed. My sister was only two years old. One year younger than me. But she had to go through the same things. I knew that and nevertheless, I secretly hoped they would leave me alone and only take her. But it was all so unpredictable. Most of the time, we were both picked out of our warm little nest and wrapped in a blankets, then they carried us to a limousine. I'm ashamed to admit that I hoped that they would take my sister, especially now, because my sister has been in a mental hospital for more then 20 years. She will never come out again. To be honest, they will never let her out because the man who has to make the decision to release her is the psychiatrist that also raped her for many years in this gang. When my sister dares to talk about what happened to her, he states she has deviant fantasies and she suffers from perverted desires . . .''

Where did we hear that excuse before? Or should I say 'cover up'? Wasn't it Abraham who said it? How beautifully he prepared the excuses for all those perverts for more then a century. Even the professional perverts use that excuse hiding their own perversions.

"So, he stays her Master and controls her entire life. Anyway, who would ever believe my sister? It is the word of a 'mentally ill patient, against the word of a 'normal' psychiatrist'! I cannot help blaming myself for my egoistic thoughts as a child. Now my sister is in that mental hospital and not me."

The abuse suddenly stopped at the age of 15. One night the violence at one of the sex parties was so serious that Kelly had to be taken to the hospital with severe head injuries. Her skull was smashed. She had to tell the doctors that she fell off her bike. The traumatized child did not dare to tell what really happened.

Kelly tells me her story in a monotone, cold, distant and almost insensitive way. She confronts me with a reality I don't want to know or accept. I'm aware that I have to be very careful and that my questions must not show any disbelief. Kelly would indisputably close herself off forever. Victims that tell their story to the world, are often confronted with disbelief and even with disgust. We don't want to believe that something like this can exist. If it doesn't exist, we don't have to do anything about it. How does one start a battle against something that is almost impossible to accept with your brain and your heart?

I would like to clear something up for the reader, so as he or she can better understand the reactions of 'professionals' in this major problematic issue:

"Sexual abuse has truly been, in Florence Rush's words, 'the best kept secret.' Although research since the 1920s has consistently documented a high prevalence of sexual abuse, the information has been largely ignored by professionals and seldom made available to the public (Salter, 1988) A convenient theory was used to explain the numbers of adult women complaining of sexual abuse as children. They were victims, not of sex offenders, but of Oedipal fantasies (Masson, 1984). Those adults and children who were acknowledged to have been abused frequently found themselves blamed for the attacks. Abraham wrote in 1972 that" . . . Female hysterics in particular are constantly meeting with adventures. They are molested in the public streets, outrageous sexual assaults are made on them, etc. It is part of their nature that they must expose themselves to external traumatic influences. There is in them a need to appear to be constantly subjected to external violence. In this we recognize a general psychological characteristic of women in an exaggerated form (p.57)"

And Anna Salter goes further:

> ". . . Throughout this century young child victims have been frequently described as 'seductive' or 'provocative' (e.g. Mohr, Turner, & Jerry, 1964; Revitch & Weiss, 1962; Virkkunen, 1975)

The clinical basis for these observations were sometimes interviews with the offender alone.

Revitch and Weiss (1962) noted that, 'We rarely had the opportunity of examining the victims of paedophiles; however, we have the clinical impression that quite often the child victim is aggressive and seductive and often induces the adult offender to commit the offense."
In a 1981 article Virkkunen implied the offender's word should be taken over the official records in a study in which the two differ as to the degree of 'victim participation'.

Under such circumstances there could be little interest in treating sex offenders. Some authors, in fact, suggested that it was the 'participating victims' who were in need of treatment. "Unlike most other sex crimes, the male offender in the case of statutory rape has not special pathology; the girl is usually more in need of psychiatric care of other attention" (Slovenko, 1971) . . ."

It is evident that in that context and with that background information, little effort has been done to really protect children against the most horrible crimes against them and their integrity. One can ask himself, without any doubt, what the 'professional profiles' of each of these 'experts' is. But the biggest crime of the last era exists in the fact that it is exactly this kind of psychopath that has been determining the actual policy for many decades and for millions of victims. If this had happened in an 'open war' as in Nazi-Germany, the whole world would have been in shock. But under the cloak of 'science' and 'expertise' the lives of millions of victims have been destroyed for ever. And still. Because still the same 'convictions and suppositions' are being instructed at universities all over the world. And still there are professionals who, from a destructive manipulation of the basics, instill their 'knowledge' on the victims and the offenders whom they have in treatment.

Very often we see that many professionals don't even know what to do with this problem and even have a major problem talking about sex. This on its own is already a real problem. How can one expect a victim to feel safe in his treatment? And how can we expect an offender to take such a treatment seriously

The conversations with Kelly progress slowly, very slowly. So many experiences are too painful to put in words. I don't insist. Nevertheless, I want her to explain to me why she didn't make a complaint to the Justice Department. She replies with resignation that it has no sense anymore. The term of limitation has passed ten years ago. Anyway, who would ever believe her when she comes forward with the names of the clients? They would fall like a bomb. She remembers all of them, but she doesn't want to betray them. She knows they will kill her or her children if she talks.

"Nobody can change the past. Nothing can give me back my childhood and nothing can get my poor sister out of this miserable institution. She doesn't even want to get out anymore. For more than twenty years everything is taken care of for her. Heavy medications break her resistance and her will and she cannot think for herself anymore. Nobody gets access to her real thinking and being. As long as she refuses to cooperate, I cannot get her back to a real normal life again. She doesn't know that world anymore. She is doomed to stay there till the end of her life. My sister has the stigma of 'a throw away child."

Many years later Kelly finds the courage to see her mother and to confront her with her past. Her mother is very wealthy now, despite her children. She strongly denies everything. Kelly wanted to know the true motives because she wants to get rid of the doubts she still has. Her parents have sown discord and doubts concerning the abuse, and these doubts and insecurity have poisoned her mind.

"Mama, you and daddy received 1.500 euro per night, to lend me and my sister out. In this time, mama! More then thirty years ago! That was a lot of money, mama! Why did they pay so much money? Why, for God's sake, do you continue to deny what you did? Tell me the truth! I have to know!"

Kelly hopes that one day her mother will tell her the truth. She wants from her mother what Mary wanted from her father: that she will ask for forgiveness. Unfortunately this wish will probably never come true. Her mother is old and sick now and maybe she won't live for much longer. As a manner of speaking, this mother murdered her two daughters.

Although these children have not been physically killed, they certainly are in the deepest core of their emotional world. Often the question rises, which are more the victims? those children who have been 'released' from their inhuman pain, or those who have to go on living with it.

Physically abused children say they'd rather be dead then to continue their life. But even for victims of sexual abuse the suffering goes beyond the real abuse. Even if they are not longer abused or threatened, they live in fear and terror. Every night many of them re-live the 'nightmare' of the past. Flashbacks scare them during the day. Depressions, psychosomatic complaints ... many try to 'kill' the pain with drugs, alcohol or medication. A lot of these children end up in the prostitution business. For some of the victims only suicide can make an end to the unbearable suffering. The need for specialized help is very urgent in this field. But even more than this help, we need to start prevention focused on the adults that abuse children in the first place. It is not up to the children to protect themselves. It is my conviction that prevention campaigns only focused on children are made by child sex offenders themselves. Who else but a child sex offender can know that a child is unable to say 'no' to an adult? I heard that so often in my office out of the mouths of sex offenders: "But the kid didn't say 'no'". I have pictures of newborn babies, raped. How do these campaign makers imagine a baby saying 'no'? And even then! Most of the sex offenders will convince, trap, and force the child anyway to get what they want to have.

It is up to society to help and protect children. We cannot expect a child to be responsible for its own safety. We teach children to take care in the traffic, but most of all the campaigns are directed to the adults: drive slowly, wear safety belts, . . .

With child sexual abuse, we do the opposite: it's the child's responsibility to look to its own safety. Why is that?

The Reaction of Society

Repression has never been a real solution to problems. It has negative consequences for the victims in the first place. Since 1991 France increased the punishments for child sex offenders dramatically. Child killers risk life sentences. The consequences are obvious. Child sex offenders that did not kill at first, will be tempted to make their victims quiet and silent and will only find a solution in killing them to obtain impunity. The victim stays the most important witness.

The law concerning child sex offences is different in every country of Europe. A child sex offender can limit his risks by offending in countries where the sentences are less severe. We'll see this later in the book.

The population stays focused. It feels repulsion to all that concerns child sexual abuse. No matter what the law in their country says. More and more parents keep their children at home. In fact children are in a kind of prison, while little is done to make the offenders aware that they are wrong and the child cannot be responsible for what the adult does. Instead of preventing the offender attacking a child, the government focuses on the child. It is not up to a child to protect himself. It is our responsibility to do so.

We need an enormous amount of courage and good will to put an end to this 'explosive' situation. We need very specialized treatment for the offenders as well as for the victims. And we absolutely need the right attitude to address the offender or the potential offender to make him or her aware that he is responsible for his acts. Not the child.

CHAPTER 3

Six Types of Paedosexual offenders

One cannot put every paedosexual act under the same name. The problem is much too complex to do so. To gain an insight into the different forms of paedosexual crimes, one needs to examine separately, every crime and what happened before the crime. It is important to talk to the criminal and to make clear to him that you know his motives and his action field. This gives him the feeling he is understood and that he can share his information with someone who does not judge him. Throughout his life, the child sex offender has to make sure that nobody finds out about his double life, because he knows that what he does is a crime, even if he convinces himself again and again that what he did was not so bad, he didn't really harm the child. It is in their nature to find endless excuses to justify what they did. He will try to convince especially himself that what he did was not that bad. The fact that he can share his story with someone else is not only a tremendous relief, but also often the beginning of an impressive healing process.

We can give a certain amount of typical characteristics to each type of criminal. Recognizing and knowing these characteristics of a person can be very important. It gives the researchers the opportunity to profile and to identify the offender. This specialized knowledge is also very important to measure the risk factors for relapse later. We know that criminals never change their 'Modus Operandi, while others can become more violent and dangerous because they do change their Modus Operandi systematically. For all these reasons it is important to separate the different categories. The division I use is based on the studies and figures of the Gracewell Institute of Birmingham and the information of Kenneth Lanning of the FBI in the USA. Kenneth is one of the best specialists in the profiling of child killers and child abductors. The National Center for Missing and Exploited Children also offered me an important amount of information.

Each of the six categories needs a personal approach. A fixated paedosexual, for instance, is different from a paedosexual in regression. Not only is their Modus Operandi different, but also their signature can differ. While the first type is only interested in children and is unable to have sexual relations with adults, the other type starts thinking of children when relations with adults don't work out as he would like it to. The causes and the dynamics of the crimes are different and it is obvious that the approach in questioning or treatment is different too.

I prefer to classify my clients in a certain category. This gives me a starting point for the therapy: I can begin my therapy with the individual, based on everything I know about that profile and during the therapy I can refine it.

A. The sexual explosive and sadistic criminal

The first group of paedosexual criminals belongs to the sexual explosive sadist. A man of this type has an overloaded personality. Violence turns him on, on a sexual level. He is mostly addicted to pornography. He can be very evil and very cruel. This type is very violent in his social environment. He is aggressive and always on the lookout for disputes and is therefore avoided by most people who do not wish to be involved in any problems. His thinking is dominated by fantasies. He has a compulsive need for control and he seeks to dominate others all the time. Power is for him indispensable. To feed this need, he will hurt and humiliate others. He does that verbally at first. He is capable of killing a child to get back at women. He does not necessarily focus on the children of the woman he wants to punish, a random child will do. The killing itself will calm him down for a while and will neutralize his anger towards women.

He is a very egocentric personality. Everything is about him, and has to be done the way he wants it to be done. He does not take into account the needs of others or society. He adores war films especially where mutilations are the top item. But you can also find him in Luna parks where he is playing war games on automats. If he reads, he reads detective stories. He collects weapons to reassure his image and to inflict fear. He looks for victims in remote areas where the risk of being seen is low. He owns an impressionable collection of hard porn and this is important to look for during search warrants.

His intelligence capacity is normal and so he is able to erase the traces of his crimes. In general he detests people. He doesn't shrink from stealing and cheating his environment. So we can say that society not only rejects his deviancies in sexual behavior, but also many other aspects of his life. He can be cruel and without mercy towards animals and elderly people. In general this type of man has a heavy criminal record.

B. The Anger Rapist

At the root of the aggression of the anger rapist lays a woman. It can be his spouse, his mother, his grandmother, but it can also be a woman who plays or has played an important role in his life. In fact he is afraid of the dominance of that woman and feels inadequate to deal with her. To escape the tremendous sense of frustration, he projects his anger on to others. He considers all women to be hostile and untrustworthy. He will behave in a way that women will reject him automatically. He will, for instance, search for an argument over unimportant things and continue nagging on about this until his wife throws him out. The feeling of being rejected guides him towards the crime he intends to commit. The rejection of a woman lights the fire, but he is perfectly able to provoke the dispute. This profile is unable to see women in realistic terms: they are either prostitutes or saints. There is nothing in between.

He reacts with childish anger tantrums and loses control when someone dares to doubt his masculinity. In normal circumstances, he is not able to rape or kill somebody. He has to be in that 'special state of mind', some kind of depression, to become dangerous. When he rapes a woman or a child, it is not the sexual act on its own that counts. He wants to intimidate, control, humiliate and hurt. It is a type of criminal that rapes women and/or children but also who is perfectly able to have sex with animals, play masochistic games etcetera.

He is a 'macho', he wants to be seen and be admired. Police officers are often appalled by his crimes because he uses much more violence than necessary to commit his crime. So they can conclude that he beats a woman up completely, while the victim was absolutely docile or paralyzed with fear and had not put up any resistance against her attacker. Or, he uses a lot of violence against someone who is physically unable to defend themselves: children, elderly, disabled people . . .

It is important to find out if this type of criminal talks while committing his sexual crime. The words he uses show his great anger and revenge towards women in general.

The anger rapist seeks his victims in his immediate environment. It is important for policemen to gather all the information they can find about his crimes to localize him as fast as possible because over time the crimes become more violent.

C. The fixated Paedosexual

The great child friend

Frank, one of my clients, frequents places where one can find children. He is the great organizer of the Santa Claus Events, arranging group travels for kids to the seaside. His whole environment considers him a saint. He deserves a medal for his kindness and his patience. You simply never see this man without children around him. He tells them stories and fairy tales, takes them to the films and to Disneyland. Nothing is too much for him. Parents trust him blindly. He is heard to say things such as: "children are so pure" and "children are so innocent".

He has his preferences: children around nine years old, but it is not really important. If they are not available, it is ok for them to be younger or older. He manipulates parents so they are never around when he goes somewhere with the children.

Frank does not cross the lines! He is perfectly able to initiate sexual games without crossing the limits. He takes pictures of naked children and gathers collections of pictures of children. In contrast with other types of paedosexuals, he does not need stress to exhibit his sexual acts. Frank has been caught when he tried to develop a network of child prostitution.

How do we describe the fixated Paedosexual?

The fixated paedosexual only gets aroused by children. He goes as far as hanging pictures of children in his bedroom. The pictures stimulate his fantasies. He can look at them for hours while he is inventing all kinds of sexual situations between himself and the children. Once he is aroused, he masturbates. This allows him to rid himself of some of the pressure he feels. Adults or peers don't speak to him on a sexual level. The fact that the paedosexual has difficulties in building relationships with adults, means he seldom has a partner. If he has, the partner cannot cope for long. His behavior is so childish and he often has temper tantrums. He feels much more comfortable alone or living with his mother. Sometimes he engages in a marriage of convenience, because this allows him easy access to the children of an earlier marriage of this new partner.

He knows exactly which child fits into his scenario. They have to be vulnerable on an emotional level as well as a physical one. His behavior is very predictable. He adopts a pseudo-parent role to mislead the victims as well as their parents. He helps the child with his homework. He encourages the parents to go out for a romantic evening so he can take care of the kids. He plans and organizes and worms himself into the family life. He wants his place in the family. When, after some time, the abuse comes to light, the parents are devastated: not only do they have to deal with the abuse of their children, but also with the tremendous abuse of their trust. Their trust will stay damaged for a long, long time. Often they really need professional help to get over this. They cannot possibly be supportive of their damaged children if they are unable to find a balance in this drama.

The fixated paedosexual has a well-designed Modus Operandi. He seduces his victims. He does not hide his 'love' for children. He talks a lot about them and surrounds himself with children. He takes his time to build up a relationship with his victims and he knows exactly how to deal with children and how to approach them. He gives them the feeling that they are very special. Children feel attracted to this and comply easily. This gives the criminal the idea that they agree with what is happening. As if these children can measure the danger they are in! As if children know what is going to happen and what the adult is really up to!

This type of offender is a very good listener and he can perfectly empathize. He understands their little children problems so well and he gives them the advice many children so desperately need. Of course he knows which child is in need of attention. Attention the child sometimes fails to get from its family. He will fill in that terrible gap with pleasure. He gives the child candy, comics and also takes them to the cinema which moves them to a safe place for him.

He dares to threaten his victims to make them silent about the abuse. For the outside world he looks a perfect functioning man. Observant people get confused about what they feel and what they see. They start doubting their observations and themselves.

When the fixated paedosexual has friends, they are in general also paedosexuals. They exchange information and pictures between each other. When arrested he will try to maintain that this is the first time this has happened to him, that he is absolutely not interested in children and in that light . . . he is unable to explain why he abused a child.

He is extremely well organized and a really obsessive person. In his home everything has its place. Documents are precisely filed in covers, which in their turn are classified in well-organized places in his office. His house is clean and tidy. He hates rubbish and chaos. Prestige and authority are very important for him. He uses this to seduce children. When he is a policeman, he can exercise his power on the powerless child. Briefly, everything is good to obtain his goal.

Some of these men who feel attracted to children are able to control their impulses. Some are able to convince their partner to take the role of a child in sex games.

D. The Paedosexual in regression

The friendly neighbour.

Robert is a paedosexual I had in treatment. He plays the part of the helpful neighbor. He helps the parents of little Rita who is six years old. The family are new in the neighborhood. He shows them where the shops, the library, the station are in the town.

"A nice little girl you have there", he says to the mother of Rita, "She is very intelligent. I know a perfect school for your little girl."

Rita's parents think this is a good idea, but they are afraid that they will have little time to transport their daughter, to and from school. They both have a new job.

"But that is not a problem!" argues Robert. "I can take care of that. I have loads of time."

Rita's parents are grateful for so much kindness and they decide to accept his offer. Robert collects Rita from school several days a week. He keeps her with him till her parents come back from their work. Soon he knows how the family functions. He knows precisely when relations between the mother and the father are not good. He learns their weak and strong points. He helps the father with little jobs in and around the house and he is a good listener for the mother.

While Rita's mother is drinking a cup of coffee in the kitchen with Robert's wife, he takes Rita with him to the basement. He has some wonderful painting-books for her. Rita's mother does not question why he does not bring those painting-books upstairs. She is not suspicious at all. Why should she be? So, Rita goes down in the basement with Robert. There the child has to first 'pay' to use the painting-books. That 'paying' means that she has to fulfill some sexual fantasies of Robert's. Rita has to take his penis into her mouth and suck very hard at it. "It is only a game. A secret game. A secret between you and me." Robert has positioned a mirror in a way that he can watch what is going on. This arouses him even more. On a little table he had set up a camera. He can take pictures of himself and the little girl naked, in the mirror.

Robert was never aggressive. Everything that happened was carefully planned. He is calculated and cunning. At first he mixed some painting-books with some porn. While Rita is looking at the painting-books she finds the porn pictures. No, she does not run away. He trapped her. The child does not understand. She's only six years old.

"Later, when you are a woman, you will do all of this too, you know. Don't be scared. This is normal. I'll teach you one or two, so you will be a little prepared when you're older. It is better that I teach you because you know, . . . there are bad men out there! Men that can hurt you, and I don't want you to be hurt. Never go with someone you don't know, you hear me? That is very dangerous. Don't get into a car with anyone."

In the mean time, Rita's mother is calmly drinking her cup of coffee with Robert's wife. They are talking. Neither of them know what is going on downstairs. Robert's wife has no idea of what her husband is doing. The little girl does not understand why her mother is not coming to save her so she decides that mother allows what is happening to her. She is looking for an explanation: she must have been a bad girl and now she is being punished.

She does not know why she is being punished, apparently for something she did not do. All these confusing things and thoughts result in psychic problems. The consequences don't wait: Rita soon has nightmares, urinates in her bed, is unmanageable, starts biting her nails, her school results drop, she flies in a fantasy world, suffers from stomach ache and is often sick.

Rita's mother does not understand what is going on with her little girl. There have never been problems before. Rita was a wonderfully happy child. She decides to go and see a psychiatrist. He does not find anything. Rita starts having problems with her sight. Her mother takes her to an eye-specialist, but he cannot find the source of the problem either. Because Rita is constantly grinding her teeth, her cheek is becoming deformed. Again a specialist is consulted. Rita has nightmares and is very rebellious towards her mother. A psychologist is consulted. For years Rita's mother runs from one specialist to another. Everybody tells her that her daughter is attention seeking. Even the gynecologist, who finds a vaginal problem, says the same. Nobody suggests that there might be a problem of sexual abuse. In the mean time the sexual abuse continuous.

Rita is eight years old. She finds the courage to tell Robert that she will tell to her parents. His reaction is typically. It is probably the reaction most of the paedosexuals have in their heads: "I would not do that. Your daddy will not believe you and he will laugh at you. If you tell your mother, I will kill her and your brother too."

The abuse comes to light by coincidence. Rita is twelve by this time. One day, Rita's mother bumps into an acquaintance from years ago, he is the father of two little boys that also went to Robert's house. This ended abruptly the day that one of the boys started to talk about sexual abuse committed by Robert. The parents of the boys immediately made a complaint at the police station. Rita's mother feels like she is struck by a lightning! Everything suddenly makes sense! She recognizes what that father is telling her: his children became unmanageable, started to urinate in their beds . . . How is it possible that she never thought of this? Why did Rita never say anything? Completely confused she drives home and questions her daughter. Rita becomes hysterical and finally admits she has been a victim for many years.

The friendship from the mother for the offender turns into an unbearable hate. The pieces of the puzzle fall into place. Reasons; why Robert suggested her child to go to that special school, why that friendly neighbor collected her child from school, why he took her to Disneyland, and why Rita became so sick . . .

The question remains: did Robert's wife know what was going on? No. It might seem unbelievable, but paedosexuals in regression are so manipulative that one starts questioning his or her observations. Robert managed to manipulate his wife so far that she was the one being treated in a mental health hospital, when she was perfectly all right. Two years she was kept prisoner in that hospital and this only because her husband was a respectable citizen above all suspicions. He had a solid job in the education department and nobody questioned that man. He continuously told her that she saw things that weren't there. At the end, completely exhausted, she started to believe what he said. He undermined her whole personality. Finally after twenty years of sexual abuse of children, Robert has been arrested and convicted to a long prison sentence.

The paedosexual in regression is the man that eventually is only attracted to adults. He has had an apparently normal adolescence. In general he is married or he lives with a partner. Alcohol can play an important role in his deviant behavior. He is not really able to give a sense to his life. His relationships are not really deep and are only superficially developed. It is only when he reaches adulthood that he begins to show interest in children. His interest grows together with stress situations from which he can no longer stand the pressure. It can be the rejection of a woman, a divorce, the loss of his job or financial problems. He experiences this as an overwhelming injustice. His frustration seeks a way out, and preferable a way without further frustrations.

At first his sexual crime has an impulsive character. He thus, is identified quite fast. While in prison he will refine his Modus Operandi. In his fantasies he writes a new scenario in which he examines how he can control his victims so they won't speak. He will do whatever he can to not be captured again.

A paedosexual of this type is unpredictable. His arousal and excitation can increase as well as decrease under the influence of stress. He does not interpret the behavior of his victim as that of a child, but of a pseudo-adult. The little girl with the short skirt watching television is obviously a challenge to him. He convinces himself that she is provoking him with her little white underpants. How on earth can a five year old be conscious of what a paedosexual is thinking? What child of that age is conscious about his or her sexuality?

The paedosexual in regression has an absolute preference for girls. He can experiment with little boys, but girls arouse him more.

E. The Sexual Rapist

Sexual rape can seem a pleonasm, because isn't rape always a sexual crime? Of course it is, but many rapes have more to do with abuse of power and hate than with sexual pleasure. For the sexual rapist, the sexual act is central.

He is unable to be assertive. He feels incompetent and weak. He is the target of harassments. The more he defends himself, the more he will be harassed. He is made to feel inferior and flees further away from reality. In his imagination he sees the forms of revenge he will take because he cannot cope with adult harassers. Bit by bit his fantasy world starts to overwhelm reality. In this fantasy world he is the winner. Nobody can harm him there. In a flush of hate he seeks an outcome to calm down his anger. Somebody will pay for his pain. Who? That does not matter. This type does attack strangers and his attacks become more violent over time. For him there is no other way of communication than violence to explain his lack of inner peace. He will experience his sexual needs and his frustration by using violence. In an extreme way he will feed his fantasies with pornography. He suffers from sexual dysfunctions, which he experiences also as lacks in his masculinity. For years he is obsessed by the idea that he is sexually inadequate. He is sure that everybody makes fun of him for that.

From this type of criminal the victim has a very good chance escaping his violence when she or he opposes the aggression. This sexual criminal is not prepared for this and runs away.

He cannot find security anywhere because he lives a very isolated and lonely life. The neighbors know him but have never had any real contact with him. He seems to have no need of anyone else and is socially so handicapped that nobody wants him as a friend. There comes a time when people from his environment discover that he is someone known by the police for sexual abuse and this will isolate him even more.

His crimes can be considered as impulsive and disorganized, also as compulsive. When his anger and frustrations are awakened, there is nothing that can stop him from acting out. He fantasizes for hours about slaves and docile women. He likes them the most in this position. But no woman wants to be his partner. He dares not talk to them in order to construct a relationship. In general this type has no car, which means that he seeks his victims in his immediate environment.

F. The Social Rapist

The social rapist finds himself better and more intelligent than the average criminal. He is proud of his criminal past. When he is not stopped, he can become a very sophisticated sexual criminal.

The social rapist is socially extremely well adapted. He is a very good speaker and demands of his environment that he is taken seriously. When he rapes a woman, he expects that she enjoys 'the experiment'. He is convinced that a woman who says 'no' in fact means 'yes'. It is her education that makes her says 'no', but in fact deep down inside, she likes it. He even dares to make a new appointment with his victim and takes it for granted that she will agree to his sexual advances, even when he is violent. He has very confused ideas and is extremely egocentric. This type wants to find self-gratification in the first place. He is perfectly able to convince himself that what he did was not rape and that the victim is responsible for the crime he committed. If she were not there at that moment, he would never have been able to rape her. So it is her fault.

This is specifically an education problem with an over-protective mother who refused to educate her son to take responsibilities for his actions. The mother of a viciously murdered young girl meets the mother of her daughter's killer by coincidence in the grocery store five days after the crime. Her daughter of nineteen had been decapitated and her head put into the sink. The criminal opened the skull and removed the brain. It was an awful crime. The mother of the killer looked at her and said in an ice-cold voice, "If you were not away for the weekend in Germany with your husband, none of this would have happened. It is your fault!"

We see here a mother who refuses to put the guilt where it belongs: with the murderer, her son. It is clear that since he was a child, she had over-protected him and taught him that it can never be his fault. It is always the other's fault if he does something wrong. The prognosis for this kind of criminal is very bad. As long as there is a mother to excuse his mistakes, he will be unable to see his own part of responsibility. The risks of relapse are extremely high.

CHAPTER 4

The cycle in the Paedosexual Crime

There are different stages in the paedosexual abuses. Some offenders pass by all successive stages. The impulsive types can skip stages without clear indications. We can see six different stages.

The circumstances that precede the crime have a direct impact on the thoughts of the criminal. In general it concerns a rejection. The death of a beloved person can be considered as a rejection. Each form of loss can be experienced as frustrating and is a form of injustice.

The experience of loss is for the offender the direct provocation to manipulate his thinking. In this stage he is seeking justification of the act he is going to commit. "Children provoke me." "What I do is not so bad." Or "Somebody has to teach them about sex." are typical expressions of paedosexuals in this stage. He has experienced an injustice in his mind and to be able to manage his lack of power or incompetence to deal with this, he wants to dominate the weaker. This gives him the feeling he still is a personality who can control his life. That he has to abuse children, he leaves out of the picture. The point is: I have to feel better. Then he will look for an excuse to justify to himself the act he is going to commit. When he does not find that excuse in his own life, he deliberately provokes disputes to obtain rejection from his environment. Then he feels misunderstood and abandoned, hurt, rejected and thrown away. These are the ingredients he needs to be in the mood to commit a crime. A small percentage of paedosexual criminals do not need to settle into this state of mind to commit a crime. These criminals say, without scruples: "I raped a kid, so what?!" They put their conscience on hold. These types of criminals are very difficult to treat. We call them psychopaths.

The third stage contains the fantasies. Most people have sexual fantasies. In general they are 'legal' fantasies and there is nothing wrong with it. They can be based on previous experiences or memories of sexual experiences or a special detail about it. Paedosexuals also fantasize. Their fantasies are 'illegal' because they are a preparation for the crimes they want to commit. Very often they masturbate while fantasizing or they live their fantasies inside while having sex with their partner. Most of the time this partner is not even aware of that. A fantasy world is very personal and intimate; in fact even more intimate than the sexual organs. One can rape someone else with force but it is impossible that someone can get access to fantasies from an individual, even when using force. When the other is not ready to talk about it, someone else will never know. When paedosexuals tell their therapist that they have been 'suddenly struck' with an impulse, they are lying. Such crimes almost never just happen. Their fantasies are steps to come to the crime. The problem is that nobody can understand the signals about the preparation to commit a crime in the head of a criminal. Fantasies are still too often ignored or minimized by professionals. That is a big mistake.

After fantasizing the criminal starts his tracking of the victim He observes children at the swimming pool, on playgrounds, around schools. He looks for a proper victim and keeps an eye on it, sometimes waiting long hours. He will look for a child that has no real place in the group. Or one that is excluded from the group. He knows exactly how this feels and he also knows exactly what this child needs: attention. A child standing against the wall of the playground. Alone. While the other children are playing and having fun. Or a child that is smaller than the others, or disabled. While he observes the child he will try to catch the eye of that child. This child needs attention and love. It feels flattered by the attention of the adult staring at him.

Immediately the criminal moves to the next stage of his planning. He approaches the child and talks to it. He understands his pain and suffering and recognizes the feeling of rejection. Hasn't he himself always been isolated? Who can better understand this child than himself? He tries to find out what the child's interests are. He is a good listener. Step by step he succeeds in isolating the child and in a refined way he will disarm the child. When the child objects and says that it has to stay with the others, the offender will state: 'it's a pity that they never let you play with them. They don't want you in their group. Do you want to come with me to see a good movie?" That's how he can gain the trust of that victim. He will act carefully and will not shock the child.

In the last stage, the child is completely isolated. When the offender finally succeeds in moving the child to a remote place, he will first try different methods of disarming the child completely before acting out. After the crime the child is overwhelmed with feelings of guilt: "You are guilty, you followed me. You wanted this so desperately, otherwise you would have defended yourself." Or "You made me do these things" or "I'm just teaching you about sex." The offender can make a compliance of the victim too. "This is our little secret, everybody has such secrets. Don't tell anybody. It is just a little game."

CHAPTER 5

Why victims don't talk

Stacey

Stacey is four years old when her uncle sexually abuses her. Uncle Tom is her parent's best friend and he often comes to visit. The abuse lasted longer than six years. Nobody ever saw anything. The uncle even abuses the child in front of other people. Nobody ever noticed anything wrong. He took the child on his lap and under her skirt he penetrates the child with his finger. During a party for instance, while he is talking and laughing with other people. He does it over and over again. Stacey's parents don't react because they don't know what is going on. She doesn't want to sit on Uncle Tom's lap. "Don't be stupid, Uncle Tom is so nice!" Her parents force her and this makes it even worse for the child. Of course Uncle Tom is taking advantage of the situation.

Stacey is almost ten years old. Uncle Tom has a present for his favorite little niece. She is very scared of that man and refuses the little bra he bought her. He wants her to put it on in front of everyone so he can take a picture of it. Her parents agree: "Don't be so shy, there is nothing wrong with this." And they all laugh. Uncle Tom gets what he wants, as always. For years parents don't see the problem that is killing the little girl. Nevertheless it goes very wrong with the girl.

When she's fifteen, she is suffocating under this heavy secret and she decides to tell her mother bit by bit. Mother doesn't know what to do with the information and feels reluctant to believe her daughter. It is not the first time she finds her daughter lying. She thinks that this story fits more in the imaginary world than in reality. The girl feels again she is not believed and she's an emotional wreck. She sees no other solution than to run away from home.

She had disappeared for more than four weeks before I was contacted by an association Payoke in Antwerp, Belgium. There was no trace of her and her parents were desperate. I start working immediately, I make a profile of the situation and I analyze the information I have. She only speaks one language: Dutch. It is evident that she will go to a country where people speak the same language as she does. She must be able to explain herself. I ask the parents to make me a list of all the countries they went to on holiday the last few years. It is important because adolescents do not just disappear like this. They do plan. France seems to be an option because of the weather and because she went there several times with her parents on vacation

Very soon I get a phone call that she has been seen in the Netherlands. She is in Amsterdam, is on drugs and has been raped by a Hell's Angel. She feels even more useless than before and sinks further into despair. A few days later she is home safely, but she is not well at all. There are long waiting lists to get professional help. The need for immediate help is paramount. The government reduces the budgets from year to year. The consequences are evident. Stacey has been arrested after having dealt drugs in her school. She has been suspended. She denies everything but nobody believes her anymore because of her 'lying' past.

Is Stacey lost to our society? Is she helped with her childhood trauma? Are there enough qualified professionals to listen to these victims? Are there enough budgets for intervention in time before things get out of control? In most European countries there is a lack of coordination of the different initiatives. Added to this as well, are the communication problems for victims, for police departments and for authorities which all seem unable to work together. There is one small crumb of cold comfort: her uncle has been sentenced to prison.

Why didn't Stacey talk?

Why did little Rita who was abused in the basement of the nice neighbor keep silent? Why do so many victims keep silent? Rita didn't speak because she thought that her parents approved. As a little girl she assumed that her parents knew what was happening and that it was the way things are. As a result she suffered deeply and could not see any possibility of revealing the situation. Little Rita kept silent because she couldn't understand what was happening and she was obliged to go and see the neighbor who helped her with her homework for school. She thought that her parents agreed with this. When she finally wanted to tell her parents her neighbor threatened her, saying that her parents would become the scapegoat of her 'betrayal'. Under this pressure she kept silent for many years, even when other children started talking about the sexual abuse by Robert. Children are very loyal to their parents. The fear that something could happen to her mama was so big that she decided to carry the heavy weight alone. It was only when people assured her that the threats were not real, that she finally started to talk.

Some children are so manipulated by the offender that they start to believe that they and not the offender are guilty of the abuse. And one does not talk about his or her own guilt. This guilt . . . you carry with you.

Even more important is the fear of not being believed or heard. This fear terrorizes the child. Very often these children have no person who they can trust and to whom they can tell their story.

Confusion dominates their thinking and acting. Little children do not even know what is happening they cannot find the words to explain. Children become convinced that they must be bad when they are sexually abused. Often they think they are not entitled to a safe childhood. They send many signals to the outside world, but that world does not notice those signals, or the signals are interpreted as bad behavior of a spoiled child. By doing this, the child again gets the message that they are good for nothing and useless.

These children are in a vicious circle. The frustrations grow into anger and the lack of understanding about so much injustice does not find an outcome. The child begins to detach itself from the outside world and to be able to survive it often starts to create a fictitious parallel world of its own where it can find some peace and safety. Because the child closes up for others, the others will start to ignore the child and this has its influence on the thoughts of the child again: the stored frustrations grow. These children are at great risk, of becoming later when they are adults, themselves the offenders of tomorrow. There are children that are so traumatized that they cannot even speak anymore.

Another group of victims is too small to express itself verbally: children under the age of three. There are rapes committed on babies of some weeks old. Such a baby is not aware of the world around him or her and nobody knows how this affects these babies now and in the future. We have seen some reactions with the little girl Mary. The only thing this baby could do is shut her mouth when something approached it. We don't know yet how to help these children.

Girls, who have been sexually abused in their childhood, react different than boys. While boys unconsciously point out towards others as the guilty ones, once they are older, girls usually blame themselves. During their puberty and as young women they mutilate themselves often, or they undertake a suicide attempt. Sometimes they have all kind of psychological complaints. They suffer from depression, are addicted to alcohol, become myth maniac or nymphomaniac and show different forms of eating disorders. Many will suffer from Borderline Personality Disorders.

Let's take a closer look at the signals children show to indicate that they are in trouble:

Eating disorders

Sexually abused girls often suffer from eating disorders such as anorexia or bulimia. Their self-image is so damaged that they want to fit the ideal image, most of all the image of a super slim woman. In general they passed the super-slim-stage long since and become really skinny. These girls are able to conceal their problem for a long period of time from their environment, because they eat with the family at the table but as soon as they can they rush to the bathroom and vomit everything they ate. Some girls conceal their skinny body in big sweaters. Their hair loses its shine; their eyes are dull with dark circles under them. They are listless and seem depressed. Parents often wave this away by thinking that this is a typical adolescent sign. Sometimes girls are admitted to hospital as urgent cases: sometimes they die from exhaustion. It demands professional help to enable them to climb out of this deep valley.

Other girls start eating until they burst. For this bulimia patient nothing is safe. They eat everything that comes in their hands: sugar, biscuits, chocolate, sausages, salt . . . Afterwards they feel miserable. They are upset by their own behavior and their lack of control. They too fall into the trap of a bad self-image. The more negative their self image becomes, the more they go on eating. They become fat and dislike themselves even more. Unconsciously that is exactly what they want. Unwanted intimacies and closer relationships are kept at a distance.

Alcohol addiction

I spoke to a lot of women of middle age with a carefully hidden alcohol problem.

Annie is addicted to alcohol. Her environment sees her drunk on a regular base, but every time again she is able to con her environment. Now she has a headache, then she is so tired or she had to take medication to calm down . . . She has been arrested several times by the police for drunk driving. I talk for hours with her and screaming she tells me that she has been sexually abused for years in her childhood. The offender was her uncle. It was impossible for her in those years, to tell somebody. Nobody would have believed her. For more than fifty years Annie has suffered from this secret. There is not a night that goes by without her having nightmares. In all these years she convinced herself that there was no sense in talking about it. It is too late now. For fifty years the little abused girl in her has been screaming and yelling for recognition and justice. To anaesthetize this child in her, she started to drink. She drinks until she faints. She hides bottles all over the house. Nobody ever sees her drinking; nevertheless she drinks two bottles of gin per day.

After several months of therapy Annie feels much better. She knows that alcohol will always be a problem for her, but at least she now knows where that lasting feeling of rejections came from.

To escape on the unbearable reality, many youngster run away into drug abuse. Some children and youngsters lose all courage and indicate that nothing matters anymore. I'm convinced that a lot of users of medication like anti-depressives are in fact sexually abused people. Intensive therapy is so much healthier and better than to construct a fictitious world via anti-depressives.

Sexual problems

Some of the abused girls have experienced that sex can be a way to obtain something. They realize that they can get favors in exchange for their body. "If you want to go out with your friends, you first have to do what I ask you . . ." said the incest father. Girls can end up in prostitution. They search for revenge for the pain that has been inflicted to them as a child. They get back at other men for this and make them 'pay'. They see themselves as merchandise.

Other women that have to cope with the consequences of sexual abuse express this in other ways. They are disgusted about everything that has to do with sexuality. They have a hard time being and especially staying in a relationship. They suffer from fear and sexual intercourse is impossible. Their sexual incompetence leads to divorces.

Patricia suffered for years from unidentifiable complaints. Pain in the back, stomach, intestines, migraine crisis, heartbeats . . . She suffered from it all. She spends most of her time seeing doctors all over the country. Her problem according to the specialists was of a psychosomatic nature. But these same doctors sent her to the hospital. She has been operated on several times, without any reason. But opening, operating and then closing would give Patricia the feeling that she was 'healed'. All this did not comfort the angry, damaged 'child' within Patricia. Worse than before the complaints came back. Finally Patricia went to see a psychologist. After some weeks, her therapist was able to get the secret out. Patricia had been victim of sexual abuse by her father in her very early childhood. The 'child' in Patricia could finally speak and with that the complaints diminished dramatically. After a few years the 'child' in her was freed.

Self-mutilation

Some victims consider themselves as responsible for the abuse. They want to punish themselves by cutting and burning themselves. Self-mutilation especially occurs with girls. They have the constant feeling that they have to be punished. They burn themselves with candles, cut deep wounds in their arms with razors, keep their hands under boiling water and torture themselves for something they are not responsible for at all.

There is another reason for this behavior. Some of the victims are so scared and traumatized that they are afraid of losing contact with reality. Experiencing pain can be a desperate attempt to hold on to that reality. If failed, they sink away in a deep, dark hole and that is the worst. They cannot find themselves anymore. They know that feeling because that is exactly where they have been when the abuse was going on. They will thus do everything in their power to NOT go there anymore. Even if that means they have to inflict pain to themselves. At least this pain keeps them real. As soon as the reason for the self-mutilation is detected a long period of healing of the soul and the body can be realized.

Often I hear adults say that it is only a way to attract the attention that youngster harm themselves. Maybe that is true, but reality is different. These people don't ask attention for themselves but for the problems they are dealing with, problems of emotional uncertainty.

There are sexual abused girls that cannot cope anymore and they commit suicide. A small amount of women cannot have children because of the childhood abuse. Very often they really want children but they don't understand why nature is obstructing it. On a physical level nothing seems wrong, but in fact emotionally they are teenagers frightened to get pregnant from their offender. Here too it is important to talk about it with a professional and look for the cause of the problem.

Abused children send out signals.

Children can communicate in a subtle way that they are in danger. Instinctively they don't like some people. We as adults are often amazed why a particular child does not want to be with a particular adult, especially because very often that adult is the nicest uncle of the family who cares so much for children. Many children feel instinctively that his intentions are not pure. People, who are good for children, even if they are severe and sometimes hard in dealing with children, do not impose fear in them. The paedosexual first 'undresses' the child with his eyes. He wants to check how far he can go with the child and if the child will resist him. A child feels that. Often children say then: "Mom, this man is looking at me so strangely.

Traumatized children show specific behaviors. Suddenly, without any indication, they start urinating in their beds; this is an unconscious way of searching for the security of the womb in the uterus. Parents are often appalled to see their child become aggressive and untreatable without any obvious reason. The child is punished for its behavior and by doing so the self-image of the child diminishes even more. Some children retract into themselves. They are quiet and look sad. When we ask them what is wrong, they often answer evasively or they take off to another room without answering. Young adolescent girls would like to stay under the shower for hours. They don't seem to be able to get themselves clean anymore. They feel worthless and dirty after the abuse. They show symptoms of anorexia or bulimia. Also at school they begin to behave differently.

They shut themselves off from the group and their school results drop dramatically. Teachers can play an important role in the detection of serious problems and behavior disorders. Punishment is not the answer. These victims need trust, patience and especially encouragement to talk about their problems.

PART II

From Sexual Abuse to Child Murder

*"Grief is a passive feeling:
one can only undergo"*

CHAPTER I

The Story of John (Part II)

Starting all over

After John's release from prison the whole family moves to another area of France. John has promised to start a new life and never to touch children anymore. In a completely new environment nobody will know him and his past. A friend of his offers him a great job where he can start right away. Very soon he climbs up the ladder and become the director of the company of wood he is working for. He earns ten times more than in his earlier job. He has his own secretary and a brand new car. The company pays for all his costs and everybody considers him as 'a great sir'. For some years everything works out fine. This is only semblance because John goes regularly to the Netherlands where he does some shopping. In fact he is buying child pornography to fill his collection.

Every morning Anne, his wife, has to masturbate him in the bathroom while he looks into his 'material'. For Anne this begins to be a routine job.

Indeed, she finds his behavior abnormal, but she convinces herself that this bathroom ritual will reduce his need for children.

John is so busy at work, making a new carrier, that he sometimes forgets his need for children. But his job also offers opportunities: he has to travel a lot. First only in France, but later he has to travel all over the world. He stays at hotels and is there confronted with his loneliness and his emptiness inside. There is also the fact that he is unable to adapt to the high demands of society. He starts to fantasize about children again in a compulsive way. The urge becomes stronger and stronger and he starts hunting. One child after another is victim of his rapes. More and more he uses violence to satisfy his needs. His methods refine. He erases all traces of his crimes. For one thing John is sure: he will never, never go to prison again, and he does not want to stop raping children. He convinces himself that what he does cannot be that bad. He has been knocking on every possible door to ask for help for his problem and nobody seems to care.

One day, John comes across little Alexander, the boy is swimming with his friends in a little river. John stops his car and observes the young swimmers. He takes off all of his clothes and joins them in the water. Of course he checks the whole area to see if he is safe. He then tries to convince the children to swim naked like he does. They are so afraid and terrorized that they dare not refuse. For these intimidated children there is no fun anymore, but John enjoys it as if he himself is a little boy. We have seen earlier that what they see and experience is often right, but the interpretation is oh so wrong. The fact that the boys stayed and that they 'agreed' to swim naked, is interpreted as agreement by John He cannot imagine that they would undress if they didn't like it. Some of the children are able to escape. This strange man, with his way of making them do things, does not seem good. Some children are too scared to run away. John rapes them all. Then he sends them away, but little Alexander has to stay. The child is five years old. He is terrified. John will abuse, rape and torture the little boy for hours until he doesn't move anymore. This was in 1987. Until this very day, Alexander has never spoken again. The prognosis for the healing of this boy is very bad.

But that is not of John's concern. He is already hunting other victims.

Michèle

John starts a sexual relationship with his secretary, Michèle. She agrees to fulfill his fantasies. Destiny is in their favor: he is asked to start a new company in the USA. Michèle will go with him. For two years, John is in heaven. He can live all his lustful fantasies on the young woman. She agrees to wear short skirts, white socks, her hair in pigtails and she removes all pubic hair and under her armpits. She plays the little girl for two years. John thinks this is going to last forever. He's wrong. He became so possessive and violent that Michèle began to be scared of him. She flees back to France. John again feels rejected. The consequences of this are evident for the children in this area of the USA.

At night he calls crying to Michèle in France, he begs her to come back, he prays, shouts, screams, promises to do better and to be nicer . . . nothing can change her mind. Michèle is clear: she does not want to come back and she does not want to see him anymore.

John dreams away while listening to classic music: requiems. Then he decides to come back to France. He starts raping many children.

More down

One night he wakes up because he hears loud police sirens, far away. The noise comes closer. He hears screaming tires and in seconds policemen surround his house. His identity is verified and they take him with them in a police car. His wife and his children are devastated. There will be a trial, but Anne does everything in her power to avoid the media. John had taken care of his past criminal record. Everything had 'disappeared'. Therefore the judge is not aware of the danger of this man and he is mild in his punishment.

John is still angry with Michèle. He claims she made him crazy. She is the one who is responsible for his explosive sexual expansions. During his trial John is perfectly capable of keeping up appearances and after this; he simply goes back to work. But there he feels that something is wrong. His co-workers act strangely. Do they suspect something? This morning his big boss asks him to come into his office. He is dismissed and is asked to leave immediately. The mother of one of the victims had warned the director. John has to give in his car and he has to empty his office. They pay him two years termination wages.

From that moment on, everything goes very quickly. John has nothing to do. His wife has found herself a job, to be away from all these problems. So he is alone at home. He watches extremely violent films all day. He does the housework while Anne is out working and during his free hours he takes his daughter's bike and goes hunting. He has no car anymore. Months pass by and the restlessness is tremendous. He sees no way out. He is 42 and he will not find another job. Nobody wants him. Even his wife has enough of it and leaves the house, yet another rejection. His children do not want anything to do with him.

One day the mayor of his village invites him to his office. He is friendly but firm: John has to take his belongings and leave the village. People do not want a child molester in their midst. John is desperate and begs: but my children go to school here! He cannot find a school elsewhere in such a short time! And what about his house, he cannot sell it in one week either! What will his wife say? The mayor doesn't care. John gets one week to leave his family, house and neighborhood. In despair he begs his wife to come with him. He does not know where to go, but alone he is completely lost. A neighbor, who doesn't know anything about John's past, offers him his apartment in the South of France. He says that John will easily find a job there. John can stay in this apartment until he finds himself a decent job. He takes his wife's car and fills it with masses of medication, porn and personal things and leaves. Alone, for a long drive of 800 kilometers.

The way to . . .

John leaves with one foot in reality and the other in his parallel world. On his way to the South he decides to deviate. He first wants to see the prison he had been locked up in some years ago. In his head he only hears requiems of Mozart. At night he arrives at his destination.

He won't remember what he did that first night. It is sure that he called his wife on several occasions. He begs her to help him. Not to leave him alone. He is so scared, so alone and abandoned by everybody. He sees the whole movie of his miserable life pass by and at the same time he is slipping more and more in his fictitious world; where nobody can hurt him. Where he is the ruler, the right hand of Hitler. He is a ruler in a prison camp where he can punish children without limits. In a flash he sees the little pink bath in which his aunt bathed his tittering adoptive sister, that awful child who stole Aunty Mien's love from him. And then his Latin teacher comes towards him with his fly open and that sick smile on his face. He is hit on his little buttocks with that stick and he can still feel the pain, the grief, the distress. He sees his mummy being raped and hit by his father. He sees his little sister in the bed next to his, being raped by his father and his friends. In a provocative way Minouche and her hippie lover step, hand in hand, past him. Aunt Mien throws a heavy crystal ashtray at his head. It flies through the air and he can still hear the breaking glass clattering on the floor. He can still see the cold black eyes of Aunt Mien. Michèle, Mister Duchateau with his stinking breath and Anne, the peaceful stream in his turbulent life. Anne doesn't want to help him anymore. Anne doesn't want to anymore . . .

. . . *the apocalypse*

The next morning John drives around, restlessly through the streets of little villages. He is looking for swimming pools, playgrounds, and schools. Everywhere mothers keep their children by the hand. He enters a bookshop and buys comics for children. He throws them carelessly on the back seat. Then he drives slowly into the little village and parks his car.

As patient as a cat waiting at the little hole of the mouse, as concentrated as a predator he waits for his prey. For hours he looks around and waits until a suitable victim crosses his path. Next to him, on the passenger's seat, he has military maps. He already knows where to go with the victim. Nobody will ever know.

John is not of this world anymore. His whole body shakes with controlled tension. Around four in the afternoon his patience is rewarded: two very young girls come skipping from one leg to the other, right towards his car. They look happy. John hates luck and happiness. When he is not happy, others don't deserve being happy either. The children enter talking and laughing into a telephone box and pretend to call someone. After their telephone game, they come out of the box and approach him while he is waiting on the edge of his seat in his car. His eyes don't relax for a second. His view has become narrow. As in a tunnel. At the end of that tunnel are... two preys.

He jumps out of his car and walks towards the girls. He stops and asks them angrily to explain what they did with the telephone. It is broken now.

"You broke it. I saw how you were playing in the telephone box. I have to make an urgent phone call and now you will take me to the nearest telephone box otherwise I'll have to punish you!"

Devastated and scared to death, the two little girls enter in his car.

There was nothing wrong with the telephone, but of course two little girls of eight cannot know this. That day it was the birthday of one of the girls. There was nothing to celebrate anymore.

Excited at the thought of what was to come, John drives the car to a remote area. There he executes his most gruesome and violent fantasies on the two little girls. These two little victims have no chance of survival. For hours, a whole night long, they are raped, tortured in the most inhuman ways. In John's head resonates the Requiem of Mozart. Always louder and louder, until he slowly comes back in reality completely exhausted. This reality smashes him like a meteorite. This cannot be true! This has not really happened! He couldn't possibly have done such thing! Isn't it so that what he just lived was just a fantasy? He hears his aunty Mien say: "But John, what are you saying again. There is nothing wrong. Nothing happened. You have too much fantasy, boy!"

He pulls the cord around the neck of the little girl who's birthday it was that day, a little harder. Again reality disturbs his world when a screwdriver gets stuck in the long hair of the girl. For a second he has doubts, should he leave her alive and save her life. But that would mean that he risks going back to prison and this time for a long time. He doesn't want to go back there. Anyway, he cannot save the girl's life and he turns the screwdriver until the girl falls lifeless on the ground at his feet. Her head was almost severed from her body.

The other child saw everything that happened and knows what is awaiting her. Just for a moment it looks like she can escape when she succeeds in opening the car window and run away. But John has seen her and he grabs her round the neck. She falls on her knees on the small path in the wood and she begs for her life. Look at that! One of his slaves is kneeling for him begging for her life! John feels superior. He actually IS God in person. He can decide over life and death. He takes the black nylon cord he specially bought for this occasion out of his pocket and binds her little hands behind her back. He also binds her ankles together. Then he ties her on the shock absorber of his car. He first has to finish with her little friend. He feels tremendously excited by the idea that she has to watch that scene. Then it is her turn. He rapes the child with different sex attributes he still has in his car and after that he strangles the little girl. Like a robot he carries the two lifeless bodies and puts them in the back of his car. He cleans the crime scene and leaves.

The Ultimate Rejection

He needs to rest and goes to the apartment of his neighbor. Everything seems so unreal. He relives the awfully scenes while he masturbates. Around five in the morning he quietly leaves the flat and sees to his despair a large pool of blood under his car. There is blood dripping from the back of the car. In panic he runs inside the building again, fills a bucket with water and quickly washes away all traces of the blood. Like a lunatic he jumps behind the wheel of his car and drives like crazy through the deserted streets of the little town. For 500 km he drives without stopping and almost ends up in a ravine. He wants to get rid of the bodies as soon as he can. But hard reality plays its game again. This cannot be true! He is unable to harm even a fly. He tries to convince himself that all of this is just a bad dream and he will wake up soon and everything will be over. How can he commit such gruesome murders on two little girls! No, that is not possible. That is not true.

He turns on the radio to distract his panic. He is terrified with those bodies of real human beings in the back of his car. They are so near him! But the radio brings him back to reality again. He hears the newsreader talking about the disappearance of two children the day before. They are 8 years old. It must be true then! The radio message makes him very very anxious and he is overwhelmed by that terrible feeling of loneliness again. He hears that the police have put up barriers and obstacles and that the public has started a search for the children. Hundreds of policemen participate in that search too. The radio broadcasts the news of the missing children every fifteen minutes. There are appeals for information and witnesses. Shaking all over his body, John turns off the radio. He doesn't want to hear this. Nothing of this is real. Aunty Mien has said it so often to him: 'you have a problem in your head'. Yes, that must be it.

Finally he reaches the place he marked on his military map the day before. He opens the back of the car and takes one of the bodies by its little feet; he holds it for a few seconds over the 70 meters deep ravine and then lets it fall down. Without looking back he goes back to his car and he takes the other child to throw it into the depth. Methodically as he is, he undressed the children before throwing them away, and he also removed all their jewellery, making identification more difficult.

Later John told me that one of the children wasn't dead when he put her in the car; she had bled to death in the back of the car.
He puts the belongings of the children in two different plastic bags and he drives another 50 km. After having put stones in the sacks to keep them down, he throws everything into a lake. Then he drives alongside a river and stops. For hours, with water from the river he tries to clean the blood out of his car. Back in the apartment he cannot turn on the radio or television without being confronted by the disappearance of the two girls. He sees their pictures on the screen and hears that the whole area is in a state of alert. He is

scared to death. He cannot escape this reality anymore. Now that he cannot deny anything to himself, it does matter what he did with the children. He feels like a hunted animal and flees to Lourdes. He has to ask the Holy Mary for forgiveness. Only she can understand how he has suffered his whole life. When he arrives in Lourdes after some hours driving, the gates are closed. The visitors' hours are over, but that is not the way John interprets this. For him it is very clear that Mother Mary has literally closed the door on him. Of all rejections he lived through this really is the Ultimate one.

He looks for a hotel in the neighborhood, throws all the medication he has on the bed and starts to take every pill one by one. With a banging head he lays down on the bed waiting for death to come, he fills the bath and hopes that he will fall asleep and drown. But that doesn't work either. He staggers through the room and looks for his electric shaver. He connects it and goes back into the water. Then he puts the shaver in the bath.

At that very moment the cleaners are in the corridor near to his room and hear a horrible scream coming from the room. They hurry in opening the door with their spare key. What they see is horrific. In the bathtub lies a completely dressed man. He doesn't move anymore. On the floor of the hotel room everything is a mess. Broken mirrors, empty packages of medication, clothes . . . The ambulance arrives some minutes later and the ambulance personnel begin resuscitation John only comes back to reality after several days. His condition is stable. They decide to transport him from Lourdes to a hospital near where he lived with his wife and children. When John is dismissed from hospital Anne doesn't want him to come home. Why she refused to allow him to come home John will only find out much later. He is taken to a mental hospital near to where he used to live.

A silk thread . . .

One day Emily is allowed to go with her little niece Nadia to the drugstore around the corner. They want to buy stickers for their books. The children aren't used to going out alone. They have to be back in fifteen minutes. That afternoon the streets are deserted. An important football game keeps everybody inside.

Emily's mother puts the cake on the table. Grandma has travelled a long way to come to Emily's birthday party. She didn't want to miss it. Emily is going to blow out nine little candles when she's back.

Fifteen minutes become half an hour. They are late. Are they playing on the streets? After half an hour the family starts to worry. Emily's mother runs to the drugstore, but there they haven't seen the children that afternoon. Her heart races: there is something wrong; Emily knew they were waiting for her with the birthday cake on the table. She had no reason to not come home.

Her mother runs home and calls Nadia's parents. No, the children are not there. They start a search. It is not in the nature of these children to play that kind of game. Nadia and Emily are happy children from a normal family without tensions. They are both good students at school. For many hours the family members search the whole area without any result. Desperately they call the police.

Immediately everything is put on hold to start the search. When evening falls they know it will be difficult to look for them. That night their pictures are on television. There is not one witness. Abduction for a ransom is excluded. The parents are not able to pay enormous amounts of money to get their children back. Nobody really suspects a crime because it is almost impossible that two children at the same time are abducted without any witnesses. The children seem to have vanished. Nobody saw anything. There is not a trace of them. Day and night hundreds of volunteers help the police in their search.

One woman saw an unknown white car that afternoon. It was parked in the street. But what can such information really mean! Hundreds of thousand people in France have a white car.

Yet, this small piece of information will accelerate the whole investigation. A few days after the disappearance of the little girls, Anne is watching the news on television. She sees the missing person notice and she hears that the only clue is a white car. She puts the information together: her husband was in the area two days ago and he drives a white car: hers. She thinks back to the desperate phone calls. She is upset and a strangling feeling of anxiety creeps in. Awful thoughts now possess her, what about his trip to Lourdes? Why did he go to Lourdes? When he came out of prison the last time he told her that he wanted to go to Lourdes to ask the Holy Mary for forgiveness! Why did he try to commit suicide?

Anne calls John's brother in Belgium and crying she tells him about her bad feelings. John's brother, who hasn't seen him for forty years, calls a friend of his who is a police officer. The police officer in turn telephones his colleague in the South of France. From that moment on everything moves very fast. Because everybody took his responsibility, they succeed in avoiding John continuing to be a serial killer. The white car: a silk thread, but even silk threads can be very strong.

John's confession

The gendarmerie in the South of France prepares the interrogation of John very meticulously, because they are conscious of the gravity of the case, they don't want to be overhasty in their approach.

First they contact John's psychiatrist. They want to have an image of who John really is and what his character is like. They understand that John is very intelligent and that he likes being in charge of a conversation. With care they choose the right policeman to do the interrogation. Eddy has several points in common with John. His mother is Belgian and his father is from France. He too has been confronted with two different worlds. He knows different languages, just like John. So he has several items with which to start a conversation. Armed with a large amount of information of the personality of John, Eddy enters John's hospital room where he is rehabilitating.

Calmly and in control Eddy takes a place on a chair next to John's bed. John looks at him with question marks in his eyes. Eddy says nothing. He smiles sheepishly. Minutes of silence pass, John feels less and less comfortable and starts to ask all kind of questions of Eddy. Eddy avoids to answer.

Finally John asks: "I suppose you're here because I made a suicide attempt, are you?"

"Why do you think that?" replies Eddy with a new question.

"I cannot see why else you are here." John sighs.

"Hmm, yes, why did you try to commit suicide? Tell me about it." Asks Eddy again.

"Why would you be interested in this?" says John roughly and turns his back to Eddy.

"You know, I tried this also one day."

John turns back to Eddy: "Why? Didn't you know what to do with your life either?"

"No, that's not it. My life was a complete mess. Nobody loved me and I felt so lonely I couldn't stand it anymore. I had the feeling that nobody understood me and so I decided one day to put an end to all this misery."

"That's exactly how I felt, man!" said John "and to be honest: I still feel so. It is sad that I survived this, but as soon as I get the chance, I'll try it again."

"My mother was Belgian and my dad was French. They fought often." Eddy sighs "I had my part in this life, you know."

"Me too, my roots are not very clear either. My mother doesn't want me and my aunt also rejected me. Now my wife has thrown me out. Women are nothing but trouble. The only thing they like is hurting men."
"Were you on vacation in Lourdes?"

"No. I was there by coincidence."

A long silence fills the room again. Eddy stays calm on his chair and stares resignedly at the white ceiling. John doesn't know how to behave anymore.

He asks himself what this strange man is doing in his room. He has to know something. A tremendous fear overwhelms him. At the same time he also feels this inner need to share his heavy secret with someone.

"Are you often in Lourdes?" Eddy interrupts John's thoughts.

"No, but in the past I had planned a visit, but I never did. I was too busy. You know how things are: a busy job, a family taking your time, well, it just never happened before, that's it."

"Personally, I feel it is important to go there once in a while. One can feel soooo relieved afterwards, no?"
"You are right" John says. "When I wanted to go for the first time, it was after my release from prison."

"Oh? Have you been in prison?"

"Yes, in 1984. It was a minor offence. Nothing serious, you know."

"How long have you done?"

"I did eighteen months from the four years I had to do."

Eddy whistles between his teeth. "Four years! That's not nothing, it must have been serious then?"

"Oh, you know, I sucked up a bit with children. Nothing serious, but you know how people are, they always blow things up."

"And now you drove all the way to Lourdes. That's quite a distance, and it is so long ago, I mean, this prison sentence it was in 1984. That's more then seven years ago, no?"

"Yes, yes, but I was not only there to go to Lourdes, no, I was also looking for a job, you understand? I stayed at a flat of my neighbor until I found a job. No, I didn't drive especially to Lourdes to visit it."

"It isn't easy anymore to find a job at our age, is it? What kind of a job were you looking for? Where is that flat of your neighbor?"

After a long moment of silence and hesitation, the answer came: "In a little village near the Spanish border. It is a very nice place and I thought I could find something in the restoration. I've only been there for two days, you know."

"I know this area well," responds Eddy "I've been there very often on vacation. It is indeed, as you say, very nice and calm there. Have you visited the little white chapel there? It is marvelous!"

Eddy approaches his goal. He feels a light excitation, but knows how to control himself.

"What Chapel?"

"Well, the one in the next village it's a wonderful chapel on the top of a mountain."

"I saw that chapel, but I didn't visit it."

This confirms Eddy's suppositions that John had indeed been in the area where the children had disappeared. He was talking about a little chapel at only twenty metres from the place where the children disappeared.
John had no reason to be in that specific village but it was clear that he had been there. Is he sitting next to the murderer of the two little girls? John suddenly realizes that he has betrayed himself and his face looks sorrowful.

"Heh! You are not thinking I had something to do with these two children are you?"

"Why do you say that now?"

"Because you are talking to me about that place and you are questioning me about the time I was there."

"Oh, no!"

Another long silence, Eddy doesn't know where to go from here. The only guide he still has is the advice of the psychiatrist who said he has to let John lead the conversation. So he waits, extremely stressed. John becomes very uneasy. He doesn't know whether he can talk about it any more.

"It is awful what happened to those children" he says, while he observes Eddy's face.

"I know" sighs Eddy again, "I really feel for the man who did this. He must really be in a living hell to do such a thing. Only people who know what pain is are able to really inflict pain on others. That is because nobody ever cared about you when you were in pain when you were still a kid. You must have been such a kid. I recognize that in you. I have known that pain also. I became outrageous about this, but there was nothing I could do. You know, when I hear your story, you must have been a very unhappy little boy and you still are. I can feel your pain."

Tears are sliding over John's cheeks. He never thought he could count on so much understanding.

"But it is no reason to hurt other children." He sobs, "I didn't want this to happen. But it just happened so suddenly. Everybody deserted me. I don't know what really happened. They were running there and all of a sudden everything became black around me. I didn't know what to do anymore. Give me your gun, so I can put an end to my miserable life. I have to save my family from that shame."

Eddy is stunned: did this man just admit he had committed this crime? Or did he just imagine John did? Eddy feels as if he has been molested. He already understood that the children are dead. He cannot allow himself to say one wrong word now. He has to be careful with the intonation of his voice and nothing in his body language must betray his disgust. Because then the conversation will end and nobody will ever know where John had hidden the bodies of the children.

800 km to hell

The worst has yet to come. Eddy knows that. Each muscle in his body hurts, but it is not the moment to interrupt the rapport he built with John. Therefore the conversation is too far progressed. It is already late and Eddy feels so lonely. He can hardly stand the burden on his shoulders. But he has to do it alone. Nobody can help him here. He'd rather be home in his bed and not have to think about this mission anymore. He doesn't want to know what happened to the girls. It makes him angry and confused.

"Where are they, John? You have to show me where they are. Are you prepared to come with me and look for them?"

"I cannot remember having met someone like you, Eddy. You are so human with me. You are a real friend."

The tension is unbearable for Eddy. He has to close the conversation quickly now and he cannot afford to back off now. The chances are increasing that John might change his mind and will not want to show where the bodies are.
"Come, John, dress you. I'll arrange a car for us. Don't worry. People like you are sick. They should be treated and helped."

Frightened to death, John asks if they are going to throw him in prison again.

"Oh, no, man. I don't think so. They will take care of you in a mental health hospital."

This conversation is costing Eddy an unbearable amount of effort, but there is no alternative. The children have to be found no matter what, so can he tell a lie in exchange for the children's whereabouts and peace for the parents?

Parents that have to live with the loss of a child have an indescribable hard time. For parents that never know what happened to their children, life is even worse. There is no way these people can undergo their mourning process. They don't even know if their child is dead. It could have ended up in a prostitution network. It could have been abducted by desperate people who so badly want a child of their own because they cannot have one. Parents absolutely need to know what happened to their child. Did it suffer? Is it still suffering? Is it still alive? And if not, where is its body? Each second of the day they are tortured by these questions. Eddy knows that. He had spoken to parents that had gone through this. He has to succeed in this mission, for the parents and for the children.

Slowly Eddy gets out of his chair. No wrong move must disturb John from this wonderful moment of strange connection between the two men. He takes John's clothes out of the closet.

"Get dressed, John. Soon your suffering will be over. I'll wait for you in the corridor."

Quietly, Eddy closes the door after him. He sighs deeply, feeling relieved. Being out of this room, just for a second, is all he needed right now. His colleagues in the corridor look at him with questioning eyes. Eddy quickly puts his finger on his lips to invite them to be silent. Nothing must disturb this unique moment. He nods his head and whispers in the ear of one colleague: "Make everything ready, he will show us where he has hidden the children."

His colleague stares at him with disbelief. Is this sick man the criminal? It is almost impossible that he has something to do with the disappearances. Based on so little evidence it is a miracle that they have found the offender. Even for Eddy it is difficult to believe, but if John can show them where the children are, he will be obliged to believe.

He informs his bosses and a car is driven in front of the hospital door. John, Eddy and the prosecutor and some men from the research department leave at ten in the evening. During the whole trip Eddy speaks with John. Nobody knows that they have an 800 km drive ahead of them. Eddy has to take care that John doesn't change his mind. John trusts him. Nobody but he can fulfill this task. At six in the morning, the whole company arrives exhausted in the South of France where the bodies of the children will be found. Encouraged by Eddy, John makes a way through the high grass to the cliff. Because this spot is so dangerous a barbed wire fence protects people from falling in. It is the spot that John had indicated with a felt-tip on his military map. Everybody understands immediately that they'll need heavy equipment to reach the bottom. A specialized mountain team is called to come in and help.

It is cold and foggy that October morning. John stares with a blank face in the distance, waiting for what will come. Eddy doesn't say anything anymore. There is nothing more to say. He is exhausted. His task is over and he can only feel relief that he doesn't have to speak to this monster again.

The brutal reality

Cords and hooks are thrown down. To everybody's shock, the cords don't reach the bottom. New material has to be brought in. Longer cords are let down. Four men prepare to descend. John is still staring at them. As if all this is not true. He cannot believe he has something to do with this. This must be a bad scene in a movie and all the others are actors. He is still groggy from the medication he had at the hospital. He has no idea what is going to happen. The hours creep by slowly. There is no sound coming out of this gaping hole in the ground. The men are too deep to talk with those on top. After five hours of hard work they bring up the first child. Everybody steps back with horror. The sight is unbearable. A few minutes later the second child follows. The unrecognizable awful mutilated bodies lie on a white blanket on the ground. John turns his head away. He is horrified. This is more then he can bear. The children have been at the bottom in a pool of water for more than fourteen days, at a depth of 70 meters. Their fall has mutilated them even more than they already were. These little bodies have nothing human about them anymore. Several co-workers turn their heads away. They vomit. Never before have they seen anything as horrible as this.

Now John is handled with brutality. He has to show the investigators where he had thrown the belongings of the two little victims. At the dam he indicates the spot where he threw the two plastic bags. A diver team comes and dives to sixty meters depth, after several hours of hard work they only found one bag. The other one will never be found.

A completely dazed John is lead to the office of the prosecutor. He doesn't understand why people make such a big deal of all of this. There is nothing to do about it, is there? The children are dead. Nobody ever worried when he told them what he was capable of doing. Nobody ever did anything to stop him from doing it, although he often suggested his real intentions. Nobody cared. Why then do they care now? For John the whole business isn't real.

For fifty long hours he will be beaten and put under pressure to force him to make a complete statement. There are some issues missing and the police want to know everything. Where has he been? Who did he speak to? Where did the crimes take place? How many children had he killed in the past? Where are the objects he used to 'experience his murdering requiem'? The file has many gaps, but one thing is sure: John is the murderer of these little girls. He is send to jail.

For the parents and the families a long process of mourning and grief, of rage and not-understanding, starts. Something as gruesome as this, no one expected. This can hardly be the work of a human being. The children must have suffered dreadfully before dying. Death must have been a relief. Still, John does not realize that these facts have really happened in reality. Why all this fuss? He wonders what these angry policemen, these judges and all these outraged screaming people outside the police building, are doing in his world. He never saw them before. They scare him. As usual he tries to adjust his world, but this time it isn't working. Suddenly there is too much reality in his protected cocoon. What was real and what was fantasy? It will take months before the brutal reality of his acts will penetrate his mind.

Emily's mother writes a letter to John. She begs him to give a reasonable explanation for what he did: "My husband is going crazy with grief. I beg you, do something. Tell us why you chose our child!" John wants to answer, but realizes that there is simply no reasonable explanation for his crimes. He asks his lawyers if he is allowed to write a letter back. He is not allowed. A few months later he receives a letter from Belgium. A father asks if he has something to do with the disappearance of his little daughter. John wants to answer this letter too, but again he is advised by his lawyers not to do anything at all.

John's life in prison

Two days after his arrest, the couple Victor and Jeanne are watching the news. They heard something about the disappearance of two little girls, but they didn't really pay attention to it. Suddenly they are shocked to see the murderer on their screen is no other than their friend John; there is no doubt because the newsreader mentioned his name. This must be an awful mistake! They had known John for over twenty years. He wouldn't harm a fly. He is the most helpful man they have ever met. This must be a distasteful joke. It takes Victor and Jeanne six months to get over the first shock. Only after that time did they find the courage to write a letter to their friend John. Now, years after this drama, they are his only friends. They strongly condemn what he did, but they assume it is their duty to support him in difficult times. Every month they send him a little amount of money. It allows him to hire a television for his cell. It is his only contact with the outside world.

Everybody wants him dead. When John is transported to the police station for new hearings, hundreds of angry people gather in front of the prison gate. They shout at him and scream to reinstall the death penalty. John can see their demented faces. Is this all about him? Because of what he has done? The whole of society hates him! But wasn't it always like this? He himself hates this world around him too, ever since he was four years old.

His cell is searched several times a day. They fear he will try to commit suicide. John writes many letters to his wife Anne and to his children. None of his letters are ever answered. He sees his face on magazine covers, in newspapers and on television.

Because his life is in danger in this prison, John is transported to another prison which is much smaller with only fifty inmates and therefore it is easier to keep control. Most of them are there because of sexual assaults. Nevertheless he is the only child killer in that prison and is forced to stay inside his cell of two meters by three meters. He can never go for a walk like the others, because of this tight security.

Some guards are human. They do not judge, they do their jobs. Others behave like real brutes. They don't speak to the inmates, they yell. They don't open doors, they are kicked open. They even put little pieces of glass in John's food. John lives his life in complete confusion. He is forced to take more and more heavy drugs because more and more awful images fill his 'screen'. Despite himself, he is forced to continue to fantasize about children and what he will do to them. He sees himself with children who are bound on a rack. He sees himself torture them to death. His compulsory masturbating goes on daily in his cell. Every night he wakes up at four. Then he hears screaming mothers and he gets cold sweats. He doesn't want to hear these mothers, but they are there . . . every night. Over and over again he hears them. To suppress this he has to take heavier drugs. One day John told me: "If only I had thought for one moment that those children had parents, this would never have happened. But it didn't even cross my mind."

On a rational level John can understand very well that his crime is unacceptable, but on an emotional level he still enjoys it every day. In his twisted mind, he is somehow convinced that he had the right to do this. Everybody has turned their backs on him. Nobody loved him. Nobody wanted him. Someone had to pay for this. With enormous relief John thinks back on his crime. "It is indeed sad for these children but there was no other way to reduce my tension" he says, while observing my reactions. Not one moment, not one second did John see these children as human beings. They were objects on which John could vent his anger and frustration which had built up since he was a baby. He is absolutely aware that he cannot live in freedom anymore because he is unable to control his impulses. Over time these impulses have become so horrible. He doesn't know where they come from and he is unable to control them.

"It feels as if I'm possessed by the devil. A human being would never do such things. Can you imagine me doing such things?" he asks me during one of my visits. Lost he stares at his shaking hands. "With these hands I did all of this. If I could I would cut them off from my body. I drag these filthy things with me wherever I go, while I know what I did with them. If one day I am released from prison, I know, it is sad to say, that I would do it again and again and again." He drops his head on his arms and sobs. His hands touch mine the tiny little table. He dares not look at me while he vomits: "You know when I see a child on television . . . I hardly dare to say it . . . I have an erection. I have to masturbate while I fantasize about the awful things I would do with that child. And yes, when I look at my hands, the images of Emily and Nadia come back and I have to masturbate. I don't want it, but I cannot help it. I have to do it. Please help me . . . help me, I beg you . . ."

Powerless, I stare at him. I don't feel compassion although I realize it must be terrible to live like that. I cannot help him. Nowhere on this planet can people like John be helped. It is like trying to bring a dead person back to life. John has passed a limit, a limit that knows only one direction. Before reaching the point of killing, he might have been helped but now it is too late. How on earth can one stop the nightmares, the compulsory impulses, the compulsory masturbations, the fantasies, at this stage? Is it really so that we have no alternatives other than killing, to heal these people?

The isolation in prison increases these impulses even more. The inmate feels the hate around him. The permanent rejection! The other inmates do everything in their power to make it clear to John that his is in a permanent position of danger. John does not know when, how and where he will be lynched, but he is sure someone will find him dead in his cell one day. The constant fear, the isolation and the rejection are the perfect ingredients to feed his fantasies.

He is ashamed of it. While he admits that he would do everything in his power to protect his sister Maaike, he admits that he gets aroused when he recalls the images of his father raping his little sister in the bed next to his. Even if he cannot recall precisely the scene he is able to see that little boy watching the sexual violence committed on his sister.

One of my clients contacted John by letter. He often talked about his therapy with me to John. John asked via my client if he was allowed to write me a letter. Although I doubted strongly that this could lead to anything, I agreed. At that time he was in prison for two years, awaiting trial. He had no idea when his trial would take place. In fact he didn't know anything. His three lawyers rarely contacted him.

John's first letter contained six completely filled pages. It was the start of a long, strange and turbulent correspondence. The urge to share the events of his life and to evaluate them with someone was very high. In the coming years he wrote almost 1000 pages. For me, a world opened, an inner gutter, a cesspool that I never thought existed. Of course I know that there are 'inner dumps' and that child killers exist. But before I met John, no one ever took me with him to his deepest depth, to his hell and surely never ever confronted me with such horrible thinking and acting.

*"Anger is an active feeling:
one can do something with it"*

CHAPTER 2

Anger is a verb

Fantasy and Reality

Unfortunately, people such as John are not exceptions. I'm convinced that the step from *psychological murder*, which is what child abuse undoubtedly is, towards *physical murder* is smaller than one would think.

Many paedosexuals are aroused when they caress and touch a child and many always want more. They also demand that from a child. Imposing a sexual act on someone who is not ready for this – and it is obvious that a child is not ready – has nothing to do with love, but everything to do with abuse of power and force. Some of the offenders are so obsessed with power and control that they want to see blood; they want to decide over life and death. Cruelty becomes part of their arousal.

Often we read in the newspapers about fathers that kill their whole family before putting an end to their own lives. The explanation for this tragedy is often that there were relationship problems or that this family suffered financial problems. Sometimes their suicide fails or the offenders do not have the courage anymore to go on with their plan to put an end to their own life.

It is strange to see that media reports, lasting over a long period of time for such crimes, are often followed by a lot of identical crimes being committed because, people who play with the idea of family murder are often depressed and they lack the imagination to think of a good scenario to commit their crime. The details of the crime that appear in the media feed the ideas of these potential killers. If he can do this, I can do this too. That is what they think. They often construct their own scenario based on what they can find in the media. Of course without the media model it is very probable that something terrible would still happen, but a well-prepared script makes it very easy to carry out the crime of murder.

There are violent people who become unwillingly murderers. They can lose all control when being violent and kill a child when it was not the intention to kill in the first place. Here also the media covers these stories with pleasure. Tensions of financial kind, problems in the relationships, frustrations, and alcohol abuse are often at the basis of this violence. Often these criminals come from a violent family themselves and have learned to use only violence to solve a conflict. Therefore history is a fertile base for repetition of violence. Here too we can see that the offender acts out on a weaker victim to expel his frustration. When a child is killed, it is important to find out if the crime has a paedosexual character (see also chapter III).

The role of fantasies

A small percentage of paedosexuals have extremely violent fantasies. While they fantasize they masturbate to release some of the locked-in tension and stress. After a while, the fantasy alone doesn't satisfy anymore and they need more stimuli to increase the sexual arousal and tension. They seek pornographic images of children to feed their fantasies. And as there is habituation with some kinds of medication, this is also the case with certain sexual tools. They need a stronger way to arouse and stimulate themselves and to keep their secret thinking world active. Because the original source of their problems has never been treated, they sink away deeper and deeper in a morass of thoughts and fantasies. Reality and unreality start to get mixed up. We saw the same thing happening to John. As a child he had already retreated into his parallel world, a safe place where he was the master. Sometimes he imagined that he was Scheherazade from the fairy tale, A Thousand and one nights and an army of slaves were at his disposal so that he could torture, degrade, humiliate as he wished. That was his way to run away from reality and to survive the turmoil in his head. The greater his despair, the more powerless he was, confronted with injustice, the more he retreated back into his invented world. This became more and more violent and gruesome and began to be a copy of a Nazi camp where he was the right hand of Hitler under whose approving eyes, he was allowed to torture hundreds of children. It is amazing to see that John needs somebody to put the blame on and especially someone from whom he could say: but Hitler was worse than me. And anyway, I'm sure if confronted with this, John would say that Hitler could have stopped him from doing what he did. But Hitler didn't, so . . . who is to blame in fact?

It seems that what he did was a result of what happened with his wife. He phoned her several times before starting his hunt. He begged her for help. I'm sure he told her what he was planning to do and she refused to help. Well, why should anybody bother then? Why isn't Anne to blame in this? She could have stopped him, but she didn't. If only she could have given him what he wanted, none of this would have happened; this is a very childish way of acting and seeing things. But on an emotional level, John is not older than a four year old. That is because he was so bruised and damaged at that age already, that he stopped 'growing up' emotionally. Children of four can be awfully cruel. I remember when I was only four we had a task at school. We all had a blunt needle and we had to make little holes on the lines of a drawing. At the end the drawing would have been cut out through the little holes. I remember concentrating hard trying to do this properly, because after all it was exciting. I remember the table I was working at, and the little chairs we sat on and even where I was sitting. But on my right side, another child (I think it was a little boy) bothered me, I suppose now that he was left-handed while I was right-handed and because of this our elbows touched constantly while doing the job. Suddenly I got so angry that I turned to that child (also four years old) and I pushed my needle into his upper arm as far as I could. Then I don't remember anything anymore. It is too long ago, but I am sure that I would have been severely punished for that awful act. The punishment must have been justified because I have no memory of this. What I do remember is that the next morning I came into the playground and wanted to play with that child and he ran away as fast as he could. I didn't understand. I was four.

At the age of four, a child is unable to make the link between his acts and the consequences of his acts. This is something that is learned or taught. It distinguishes us from animals. But if nobody had corrected me and punished me, I probably would have continued with this behavior. In fact a lot of the children have several criteria matching the borderline personality disorder. The nine criteria are:

1. Transient, stress-related paranoid idealization or severe dissociative symptoms
2. Inappropriate, intense anger or difficulty controlling anger (e.g., frequent displays of temper, constant anger, recurrent physical fights)
3. Chronic feelings of emptiness
4. Affective instability due to a marked reactivity of mood (e.g. intense episodic dysphoria, irritability, or anxiety usually lasting a few hours and only rarely more than a few days) (Dysphoria is the opposite of euphoria. It's a mixture of depression, anxiety, rage and despair)
5. Recurrent suicidal behavior, gestures, or threats, or self-mutilating behavior.
6. Impulsivity in at least two areas that are potentially self damaging (e.g., spending, sex, substance abuse, shoplifting, reckless driving, binge eating).
7. A pattern of unstable and intense interpersonal relationships characterized by alternating between extremes of idealization and devaluation
8. Identity disturbance: markedly and persistently unstable self-image or sense of self
9. Frantic efforts to avoid real or imagined abandonment.

(See: Stop Walking on Eggshells. Paul T. Mason, M.S. and Randi Kreger ISBN 1-57224-108-X)

Observe young children and you will see that at least five of the nine criteria are present. They grow out of this with age and education. Older people that match five of the nine criteria are diagnosed with Borderline Personality Disorder.

People like John never grow out of this because he hasn't been educated properly since he was born.

Now, if we compare the nine criteria with the criteria of a criminal psychopath we will be amazed:

1. Superficial charm and good 'intelligence'
2. Absence of delusions or other signs of irrational thinking
3. Absence of 'nervousness' or psychoneurotic manifestations
4. Unreliability
5. Untruthfulness and insincerity
6. Lack of remorse or shame
7. Inadequately motivated antisocial behavior
8. Poor judgement and failure to learn by experience
9. Pathologic egocentricity and incapacity for love
10. General poverty in major affective reactions
11. Specific loss of insight
12. Unresponsiveness in general-interpersonal relations
13. Suicide rarely carried out
14. Sex life impersonal, trivial and poorly integrated
15. Failure to follow any life plan.

(Cleckley, Hervey – psychiatrist)

Robert Hare (Clinical Psychologist) describes psychopathy as follows:

« A social predator that charms, manipulates and ruthlessly ploughs their way through life, leaving a broad trail of broken hearts, shattered expectations and empty wallets. They are completely lacking in conscience and feelings for others, they selfishly take what they want and do as they please, violating social norms and expectations without the slightest sense of guilt or regret.

Signals

Criminals try to draw the attention to their problem in many ways. One of the most significant signals is kleptomania.

Kleptomania differs from other forms of stealing by the fact that the criminal has no real intention to enrich themselves, but because they need to feel the fear that goes with the commitment of the crime or the felony. Before, during and after the stealing, the fear to be caught is so huge that the criminal is catapulted brutally in reality. He needs that to not get lost in the labyrinth of his black thinking. He doesn't even need the object of the theft: he often gives it away or he throws it somewhere after leaving the shop. During my research for child killers I realized that kleptomania is often an element that announces more serious crimes. It is important to look for the why when an adolescent is caught when stealing something useless. Professionals have to question the youngster to find the underlying motivation and to find out what is going on in his/her mind. Asking questions about the fantasies will open doors to make it possible to talk about problems. The suffering child or adolescent will rarely talk from his own initiative, so that has to come from the professional. Once the problem is located, good therapy will prevent the adolescent from sliding into more awful crimes.

It is obvious that someone will not automatically talk about his or her fantasies. Fantasies are very private. The initiative has to come from the police psychologist.

The future killer will also try to make clear that his life is in chaos, on less obvious grounds. He knows he is a danger for society but he has not the social skills to talk about it and to convince people that he might become dangerous.

One day John rushed to a psychiatrist and told him he had awful dreams and fantasies about torturing children. He was scared that one day he would step into reality and really commit such crimes. The psychiatrist was confident that nothing like this would happen. Fantasies are only fantasies, was his idea. He sends John away with medication to reduce the sexual urges.

John explained to me that the danger wasn't in his 'pants', but in his head. He had the feeling that he got 'orders' from a twist in the nervous system of his mind. 'Orders' he had to execute. "I had no choice" he said, "It felt as if I was programmed to kill."

The medication of the psychiatrist missed every outcome and that convinced John of the fact that it was not that bad to have such fantasies and even to live some of them in reality. Even his psychiatrist reinforced that conviction because he didn't take John's complaints seriously. Some months later, the urge to kill children became so intense that he knocked on the door of a monastery. He was desperate. He wanted to be locked up to come to his senses. He hoped he would become himself again in a safe and especially calm environment. Unfortunately the abbot sent him away. He had to put his name on the waiting list. But for John it was really urgent. He couldn't wait for months!

Realizing fantasies

Child killers fantasize about the way they are going to kill their victims. After the murder they fantasize further and then they masturbate. I had several clients with dangerous fantasies. Like most of the professionals I underestimated the seriousness of such fantasies at first. I wasn't able to link them to real murders. Only after I had those serious conversations with John, did I begin to change my mind about it. Thanks to him it became clear to me that violent fantasies play an enormous role in the commitment of the crime. Something as logical and obvious surprised me. To make this more understandable I'll use a metaphor to open up this 'revelation'.

There are people dreaming one day of opening a shop with trendy clothes, For some, only the idea comes in their minds from time to time. But they don't do anything with it. Others think about how they would decorate their boutique, which style of clothes they would sell, how they would name their shop and how to finance it, yes even go out looking in which street they would like to open their boutique. And of course they try to imagine how happy they would be if they could ever realize this project. But they too, only dream and never realize their dreams. A third group of people go through the first two stages and even one stage further. They document themselves, really go out looking for a location and start their dream boutique as they have fantasized about for many years. They realize their dream.

With a paedosexual who becomes a child killer, it is not different, only he does it in a much more extreme manner. What I want to say by this is that such crimes never happen just like that. A child killer or a paedosexual will fantasize for a long time over what he wants to do. Although they will deny it when questioned at first, after a while and when they are more confident they will admit that this was not just 'something that happened I don't know what got into me!' Of course a lot of people fantasize about sexual abusing children, but will never do it. They belong to the group that occasionally dreams and does nothing with it.

When somebody opened a boutique and now knows how to do it, it is not such a difficult thing to do to develop further: they can open a second shop or even a chain. Unfortunately we can make the parallel with the paedosexual child killer. The logic is that when the paedosexual criminal once became a child killer, he will probably do it again. He needs to relive the excitement and the joy he felt the first time. The first time he still had to deal with fear to failure. While preparing his second murder, this fear isn't present anymore. After all, he succeeded his first crime without having been caught, why should anything go wrong now?

And just as someone that has to manage several boutiques and sometimes loses track of what is going on, the child killer too will sometimes lose control of what he is doing. He becomes scared because things are getting out of hand. He fantasizes about all the children he killed and about the children he is going to kill in the future. In the meantime he has reality. The police are tracking him. He feels obliged to follow up his crimes because there is always a possibility that someone has seen him with the victim.

CHAPTER 4

The Role of Pornography in Childhood

Sexual fantasies and pornography lay in each other's extension. Therefore it is important to examine a bit deeper the importance of pornography?

Pornography has its defendants. Many eminent experts doubt or deny the link between pornography and crime. Everybody, somewhere in his childhood, is confronted with porn, but don't become criminals. It is the same story for violent books and films.

I want to come back to the awful crime committed on the little boy James Bulger, who was killed some years ago in England. The murder had been committed by two children aged ten. All ingredients from the horror movie *Child Play* were present in the murder and both children saw that movie some hours before committing the crime.

My experience in working with dangerous criminals showed me that many ideas for the crimes have been taken from films, pictures, and books.

The murderers find completed scenarios. Those that arouse them can be put into reality right away.

Not all people watching pornography are doomed to act out. But we can see that people, who have been severely damaged in their childhood where they were often victim of abuse, watch this porn compulsively up to three or four films a day. This is not normal behavior anymore. Isn't it so that porn is used here as a way of increasing the frustration and the fantasies of anger, rage and revenge with material from the movie? This creates excitement and new tensions, from where some seek to get released by acting out in reality.

The FBI often finds tremendous amounts of pornography at the houses of sexual criminals. It is not so that every porn watcher becomes a child killer, but it is so that many child killers are porn addicts.

The last few years the media reports the existence of the so-called 'snuff films'. These are videotapes where an unbearable amount of horror is demonstrated on children. Not only children but also women are tortured and martyred until they finally die. In the whole of Europe police departments have confiscated such tapes. This information is seldom reported by the media. The material is aimed at a richer class of people. They can cost up to 50.000 Euros per piece. Some perverted and violent clients pay film companies to film their violence with children and even the murder of their victims. Of course such videos cannot be bought in normal video stores. They exist in closed circles and are intended for a select public. It is a horrible reality from which we cannot close our eyes. Fortunately this phenomenon is rare, but it is increasing as more and more of these films come from China, Russia and Rumania . . .

John remembers that when he was ten he was watching television, it was a western movie and he saw a troop of rangers hunting a squaw. When the men finally catch the exhausted girl, they undressed her, tied her to a tree and raped her. The scene shocked the ten-year-old John, but the disgusting images also, as it happens so often with traumatized children. These disgusting images become a steady part of his fantasies. On the one side he felt sorry for the poor girl, but on the other hand he felt aroused. The fear on the face of the humiliated victim excited him without limits. Two opposed feelings, disgust versus pleasure, manifested at the same time. He was then already in a stage where he has to pull himself back to reduce the tensions by masturbating compulsively and even that provoked again contradictory feelings: guilt and release.

Since he was an adolescent, John bought masses of child porn when he was in the Netherlands. As an adult he often went there to complete his collection with sexual attributes like whips, geisha balls, handcuffs . . . Whatever he saw in the porn films he tried out on his secretary Michèle. It is true that this porn was not the direct source of his deviant behavior but that John fed his fantasies with it, is without any doubt.

On several occasions in his life, John burned all his porn material. He also hoped that his inner devils and evil would go up in smoke and vanish.

"Children not allowed"

The influence of pornography on children is seriously underestimated. The love act is thus easily linked to violence, suppression of women and humiliation, by children and young adolescents. I once visited a family where the father was watching a porn movie on television in his underwear. On his lap he held a baby of fifteen months to which he was giving the bottle. Next to him sat a little boy of six and on the back of the couch sat a girl of eight playing with her dolls. On the floor, at his feet, a little boy of five was staring wide-eyed with a pale face at the screen. All kinds of things went on in that little head of his, but what precisely, I couldn't figure out by just looking at him. I asked the man to turn off the television because little children were in the room. He answered that children do not understand such things and that most of the time they don't watch the whole movie.

Indeed, children don't understand what they are seeing. This means that it is even more so dangerous to expose them to perversities and violence as one sees in porn and horror films. Often children suffer from nightmares wherein parts of these films they saw but didn't understand, come back. Children cannot be raised in an atmosphere of fear. They have to feel safe and loved to be able to grow up to become strong, harmonious adults. When they have to permanently look for examples of all kind of strange and scary situations, they cannot open themselves for more educating issues. They keep on searching for balance. It doesn't help to write on videotapes and DVDs:

not allowed under the age of eighteen. It should also state "Not be seen by children under the age of eighteen." It is absolutely necessary that adults be sensible. In the living room the control isn't always good. Parents too often leave this porn and horror material lying around and children often know how to use electronic material much better than their parents.

"Anger is transformed grief."

CHAPTER 5

Profiles of Child Killers

There are two major categories of child killers: the impulsive type and the methodical type.

The Impulsive Type

Profile

The impulsive type is manifestly not adapted to social life. Social relationships are almost non-existent for this type. Building up a relationship with an adult partner is way too difficult and scary for him. He is in general single and lives alone or with his mother. His environment finds him a little bizarre. People tend to give him a wide berth because they don't know exactly what to think about this person. Sometimes one hears comments like: one day something is going to happen with that man

He seeks his victims for an impulsive attack, often as a result of a negative experience, like an argument with an adult, the loss of his job, a setback, the death of his mother . . . The impulsive type experiences this as a personal injustice done to him and therefore he needs to vent his anger on something or someone.

He doesn't prepare his crime; he leaves his home in a confused state of mind and hunts for a random victim. This can be an adult, but also a child. He will rape and eventually kill. He doesn't care about the traces he leaves behind. Without mercy he will cool down his rage on this person who has nothing to do with his problems at all, but was only in the wrong place at the wrong time if not stopped quickly, this type of criminal can make a lot of victims.

To explain how the evolution of the state of mind of such a killer works, I'll give the next comparison.

Charles works at a newspaper enterprise. It is hard work and it surely is no nine to five job. He regularly has to work overtime to get his job done. He does what he can. It should be not more than reasonable that his boss is satisfied with Charles' work and the fact that he is a motivated employee. It would be nice if his boss would sometimes show some respect and encouragement. But Charles' boss is not like that, most of the time he is in a bad temper and unreasonable. How often did he yell at Charles unjustifiably?

Just when Charles thinks that this time he really did give the best of himself and has earned a little sign of appreciation, his boss starts to yell at him: "Do I really have to pay you for this?!! I could better do it myself! You are worth nothing! You don't do anything and where the hell did you put that file again? Why isn't it finished yet? Look, if you go on like this, I'll fire you, understood?!"

The whole office is as quiet as a mouse. Everybody is looking at Charles. He blushes with embarrassment. He could burst into tears. Rage and powerlessness tighten his throat, but he cannot express these feelings. This man is his boss and his livelihood depends on him. Enraged Charles leaves the office. Every second his rage swells. Like a lunatic he drives his car through the dense traffic and boiling with anger he comes home. There he let his tears fall. Self-pity and frustration overwhelm him at the thought of the unjust way he has been treated. His eyes glance around in his apartment and suddenly he grabs the most precious object he has, a beautiful antique vase, and throws it against the wall. The vase breaks into thousands of pieces on the floor. Through this one gesture, Charles has released all the energy that had built up over many weeks. By doing this, he is able to harmonize the balance and he finds himself in an inner state where he feels safe again. While he is observing the chaos around him, he doesn't feel regret or anger. Justice has been done and this gives him a good feeling. It is a shame for the beautiful vase, he really loved that vase, but even while he is clearing up the room, Charles can only taste the feeling of repayment.

Years later Charles sometimes talks about that awful day with friends. He tells it as an anecdote to show that the destruction of that vase made him feel so released. It was not the vase that was responsible for his angry outburst, his boss was. He just had to project his frustration on something else because he couldn't find an alternative at that very moment. If he had yelled at his boss, he would have lost his job and then he would end up in a negative spiral: losing his job means not being able to pay the rent, means being on the street, having nothing to eat etc . . .

Impulsive child killers experience the same on a much higher and extreme level of course. They too find it a shame for these beautiful children, but my God, this horrible act released them from so much accumulation of suffering in the past when they were unable to find solutions in a normal way. This is the result of the damage in their childhood and the lack of skills to resolve a problem in a social way. But just as Charles, years later, thinks back with a sense of satisfaction at the broken vase, the child killer lets the feeling of satisfaction precede the sense of regret for the child he threw to the ground in thousands of pieces. He too associates his crime with feelings of boundless release. Each time he gets frustrated, he will think back at his crime and masturbate to reduce a build-up of tension. But unfortunately after a while, this will not suffice anymore and the criminal will feel the urge to kill again.

The impulsive type will go through different stages before going over to the killing. The psychological deformation starts in early childhood. The basis is a traumatic experience or the consequences of a permanent emotional pressure by an ultra authoritarian mother or father. As a child he never learns to function in an independent manner and he is unable to develop his proper personality. As a young child he also has exaggerated fantasies which he adapts with stronger stimulus in his adolescence. The stronger stimulus is violent videotapes and literature. When the impulsive type finally goes over to murder he always does that in a very shocking way. It is his purpose to hurt society as much as he can. That's why he wants the body to be found. This too is part of his secret fantasy. He wants to see and experience the disgrace and the horror of this society. He enjoys their reactions to the violence he, and only he, is responsible for. This is his spectacle!

It is also important to mention that the impulsive murderer seldom prepares his crime. He doesn't choose a murder weapon. Mostly he kills his victim by strangulation because he likes the personal contact with his victim, or he uses what he finds in the surroundings of his crime to kill the victim. It is thus quite easy to identify the type of killer at work because of the traces he leaves behind (if not erased by the weather conditions or the finders of the body like witnesses or policemen) and the sloppiness of the crime scene. It is crucial that nobody touches the body or other things at the crime scene. This could make the profiling much more difficult, because some indication which may seem of no importance to normal people, but are in the mind of a damaged criminal. These indications can give us an idea of what is going on in his mind and his fantasies. And very probable these indications can be found in previous and forthcoming crimes.

The impulsive type is easier to trace than the methodical type. He is often known for his psychotic behavior. He is in such an unstable state that he is probably unable to drive a car, let alone get a driver's license. He is unable to adapt and just wanders around. If he has a job, most of the time it is one where a lot of physical force is demanded. He is unable to keep a job for a long period of time. He has no friends and there is hardly a family structure for him. He lives in the immediate area of the crime or he has lived there in the past. Sometimes his crimes take place in the immediate area of his workplace. After the first excitement of his crime and the reaction of society, he seldom goes back to the crime scene. It doesn't interest him anymore. When his anger is reduced, he goes on with his life. Sometimes he cannot keep his mouth shut and boasts about what he is able to. When drunk he can betray himself if people understand and interpret his words in the right way.

An example: the disappearance of little Kevin

In April 1989 the nine-year-old boy Kevin, disappears from a camping site in the South of France. Kevin is on vacation with his parents and his brothers. After dinner he is allowed to play outside the tent, but he has to stay on the camping area. Why Kevin left the camp site will remain a mystery forever, but it is sure he was seen at the entrance of the camping area. Around seven at night a lot of people walk in and out the camp site. Little Kevin stays at the entrance when a car stops. While one man stays in the car, the driver gets out and asks Kevin for directions in French. Kevin doesn't understand French, he is Belgian. He cannot answer. The man becomes enraged and drags the child into the car. It only took seconds. Nobody saw anything. Everything happened unbelievably fast.

Some time later, Kevin's parents were worried and they start a search in the area. Some hours later the police are alerted. The agony begins. Anxiety, searches, hope, despairs . . . Woods, lakes and fields are minutely screened. The child seems to have vanished.

A few months later the body of the boy is found by two walkers in a wood at 14 km from the place where he disappeared. His little body has been partly damaged by wild animals. He lies on his face and is nude. But the body has not been concealed. Everything says that the criminal took the child in a car. How otherwise, could he have transported this child over such a distance without having been seen? All traces and indications show us a pattern of an impulsive type of murderer. We are thus sure he lives alone, has a criminal record and/or a psychiatric file and he is antisocial. On top of this the impulsive types, as said before, are so chaotic in their thinking and acting that they are unable to drive a car. The murderer must have had an accomplice. By this system of deduction one can reduce the group of possible suspects. For over five years the investigation goes nowhere. The parents decide to give their case to a television station (Témoin n° 1 – Witness n° 1).

A reconstruction of twelve minutes leads to amazing results. A witness remembers she saw a man hanging around and hitchhiking. Thanks to her description the police were able to identify him. Francis Heaulme is definitely an example of an impulsive murderer. He was already jailed for the strangulation of woman at the other side of France. The police interrogate him concerning Kevin and immediately he admits he killed the boy. He also gave so many precise details that only he can be the murderer.

In the mean time he is convicted for more than ten murders all over France. He didn't serve his country in the military service, lives alone, wanders around in France, has no known address and was in treatment in a psychiatric hospital at the time of the murder of little Kevin. He started killing some days after the death of his mother. He was never able to accept this death and felt it as an injustice done to him. He cannot drive a car. A friend of his is his accomplice, because he did nothing to stop the killing and he never reported the killer of Kevin to the police. In this he is also responsible for the many killing after the death of Kevin. He is also compliant for helping getting rid of the body. Kevin was sexually abused and later killed in an indescribable manner. Francis Heaulme also killed two little boys in a rage. He beat them to death because he had the feeling these boys were making fun of him. They were only 7 years old. For this crime another young boy of fifteen had been convicted and sentenced to a lifetime sentence. The police were overzealous in their haste to resolve that horrible double murder that they needed a criminal, no matter what. They have put the boy under so much pressure that finally after two days of questioning without drinking and eating or authorized to go to the restroom, the boy confessed. After sixteen years, France had to release him because he was innocent. They had to pay a lot of money for that mistake.

The Methodical Type

The methodical type is much more intelligent than the impulsive type. Mostly he is situated quite high on the social ladder. He is the one who is involved in all kind of social activities in his town or city. He organizes parties for Christmas and youth camps for children. He is very appreciated by his environment. He is often married, has children and is above every suspicion. He is a respected citizen and will eventually be the last person who will be suspected of paedosexual activities or child murder.

Nevertheless the methodical type has a major problem of which the outside world is not aware of. Just like the impulsive type he experienced all kinds of traumatic events in his childhood. He built up a lot of frustration during many years. In general serious child maltreatment and child abuse are at the root of his problems. Again a very authoritarian mother and a weak father or a violent father and an overprotective mother have made up the picture in his life. With his mother he has a love\hate relationship. These ambivalent feelings for his mother are based on the ideal image he has of what a mother should be: loving, tender, protective, warm and full of understanding, comforting and patient when necessary, and if possible encouraging for her child. That is the mother he always wanted to have. Unfortunately, his mother is nothing like this. On the contrary: she is an example of impatience. She is violent and isn't scared to use her fists to hurt the child even when there is no reason too. She vents her own frustration on her child. Hysterical, she runs through the house, her child hides in a safe but lonely place to find rest. He is scared of her but he needs her. He needs her love and caring. In his cocoon of pseudo-safety he starts to build a new 'world'. For hours he can sit, his eyes closed, in a dark closet. Behind his eyelids he projects his rage on a screen. Later he will turn off this 'movie' hundreds of times in his head. One day he will grab the 'vase' to vent his frustrations and anger. He will enjoy the effect on society and he then will retreat into his 'dark closet' and wait for safer times to come out.

This type plans his crimes for years. At the start he goes through the same stages as the impulsive type, but his fantasies are much more calculated and planned but also more violent.

When he arrives in a stage of killing after several violent assaults on children, he will be very upset about what he did at first. He tries to convince himself that he couldn't have done this because he is not the type to do such horrible things. He knows the difference between good and bad very well, but he chooses to do the bad. During several months after the crime he will be in a passive state and will relive the crime in his fantasy, while he masturbates. But after killing a second victim he doesn't feel anything anymore. No compassion, no fear, no doubt. From that moment on he will feel indifferent and without mercy for his victims. The cooling-off period will become shorter and shorter between each crime. He will attack faster and faster.

When the man is not caught, he will become a serial killer. But catching this type is the major problem because the methodical type is so well organized; he knows beforehand where he will dispose of the bodies. This facet of the crime is part of the fantasy. Excited he will first look for a place where he can conceal the body after having killed the victim. Only after that he will go and hunt for a victim. Investigators don't find a trace of the abducted child, which of course makes it difficult to resolve the case: no body, no crime.

When we have to deal with a methodical type we first have to find the criminal before being able to find the body. Only he knows where it is. The impulsive type would never work like this. His circle of explosive violence is too fast and too urgent to plan it out beforehand. The methodical type builds for months to complete his cycle. He is able to drive for hundreds of miles to find a victim but also to hide it. This type seldom has a relationship whatsoever with the victim. This makes research even more difficult. Because he has not a bond or relationship with the victim, nobody can give clues about who he can be. This type needs urgent professional help to break his cycle because on his own he will never stop killing. Not even after twenty years of prison.

The methodical type feels disgust in touching the victim to kill it. He cannot stand personal contact. So he is prepared. When he decides to go 'hunting' he will take his kit with him. The objects in this kit show the total alienation between the criminal and his victim. It also shows the total lack of humanity between both. He will take care no traces will lead to him. The objects he uses vary: cords, knifes, guns, sex attributes . . . John has all characteristics of this type of child killer.

Whether we talk about the impulsive or the methodical type of criminal, in both cases it is not the sexual act in it that causes the highest arousal, but the need to control and dominate, to humiliate and to show power towards the victim. Because many of these criminals have been dominated and humiliated as children, they are unable to see themselves and most of all their victims as human beings. A child is an object for them, and objects have no feelings. The paedosexual wants to calm down the crying child within himself. The 'object-child' is a way to satisfy his needs. He has serious problems in constructing adult relationships, but he knows very well how to control children. The offender thus takes revenge on the next generation instead of the previous, the one that is responsible for his pain in the first place.

Signature versus Modus Operandi

The psychopath in general presents outwardly as a very friendly individual, disarming with smiles and affability. But their criminal mind is proactive. They have already sized up their subject as target or prey before they even make their first introduction. Their high to superior ranged IQ working overtime in the background of every subsequent interaction to get their intended victim to reveal their vulnerabilities. And this superficial veneer of personality, the mask of smile and gentleness, allows them easy access to their victim population of preference.

– Their charm is superficial, one of the points in the characteristics of the psychopaths.

Psychopaths in general have this ability to develop superficial behavior, in fact as many of us can. The difference with the psychopath is that they are highly convincing, where other individuals and criminals fall short. The typical psychopath will seem particularly agreeable and make a distinctly positive impression when he is first encountered. In fact this is a behavior that these criminals have learned by watching others and by the success others obtain by their behavior. While normal people do not act a feeling, but act as they feel, this is not the case with psychopaths. They will watch a movie and learn how to behave to contact a girl, a child or a potential victim. They know that by yelling and being aggressive at the first encounter, they will not succeed. But if they are being friendly with a woman, it doesn't mean they like the woman. It only means it makes it possible for him to look for weak spots and even to know more about her daily life. By knowing this it gives him the chance to find a perfect place and time to rape and kill her if that is his intention.

These types wear a mask of sanity, but are highly mentally insane.

In other words: these people's tools are lies. Truth has no social value to the psychopaths. They will use whatever tools they perceive necessary in order to achieve what it is that they desire.
And as Dr. O'Hara states: "*Good liars are good judges of people*"

– The psychopath is unreliable, untruthfully and insincere.

Despite early impressions that psychopaths may give suggesting that they are a totally reliable person, it's not long before they demonstrate their capacity for marked unreliability in many situations. He might be reliable for a long period of time, but he cannot hold on to this because it is not coming from inside what he wants to do. He needs these skills and tools to approach a victim. Of course this way of behaving makes people think that he cannot always be reliable. This is the person that looks you right in the eyes and even if he is caught in shameful and gross falsehoods, finds it easy to speak of his 'word of honour, his honour as a gentleman'. He even shows surprise and vexation when commitments on such a basis do not immediately settle an issue.

– The psychopath is unresponsive in relationships

Psychopaths demonstrate outward social graces very easily, and may gain inordinate respect, admiration and gratitude while maintaining a lifestyle that inwardly hurts themselves and those around them. They may be an occasional volunteer of some kind, may help an injured animal once in a while, may help deliver 'meals on wheels' to the elderly, or may dress up as a clown for children. But these things are outward behaviors exhibited to facilitate access to some people. They are not benevolently motivated.
In the mean time, the psychopath fails to be truly responsive in interpersonal relations; he cheats on his wife, he forges cheques in his parent's name, and he is prone to sudden violent, unprovoked outbursts with very little agitation. He may appear on the surface to be a humanitarian of the first order. But usually this appearance is a total deception.

– The psychopathic criminal is pathological egocentric and incapable of love.

It's evident that psychopaths are not incapable of displaying affection for others. As *Chleckley* (psychiatrist) puts it, psychopaths are clearly capable of casual fondness, likes and dislikes, and of affecting reactions that manipulate others into doing things that gratify or stimulate them. But it's very important to note that while a psychopath can skillfully mimic believable levels of love, devotion and affection, the true motive of the psychopath is not the well being of the lover, spouse or child that receives this apparently benevolent attention; the true motive behind this behavior always serves the gratification of the psychopath's needs.

– The psychopath lacks empathy

The psychopath, who has no conscience towards the feelings of others to guide his behavior, is not encumbered by the internal conflict between good and evil. It has been argued that most psychopaths in general lack the ability to take the perspective of others and therefore do not have access to that information in their decision making process. So in essence they lack the basic building material for a conscience. They do have the (certain) basic building material for a conscience, they are able to understand how others feel and they know the consequences of their harmful behavior, but the value that they place on this information is in terms of how they can use it to achieve for themselves.

There is a difference between empathy and sympathy however. In my experience in working with psychopaths, they do not lack empathy but they do lack sympathy in the sense of compassion. Most psychopaths know exactly how it feels to be humiliated and hurt physically and that is why they do it: to hurt the other as much or even more than they have been hurt themselves. What they do lack is sympathy. The victim can do whatever it wants to get some compassion to make him stop hurting her or him, he will not stop. Because he enjoys what he is doing. It gives him great satisfaction. He too probably has begged and prayed one day that the hurting would stop, but nobody ever listened to him. So why should he listen to others. He chose to hurt. see people as objects to be used for his own gratification. The more the victim suffers, and is in pain the more the sadistic psychopath will love it.

He also knows that he is the one inflicting that pain and fear and that gives him the 'god like' feeling' he so desperately wants.

A lot of people confuse empathy with sympathy. But it is not the same.

While in prison, the rejection is complete. The criminal has time to fill his mind with frustration and anger and transform it into fantasies. Also will he reexamine his crime and try to find out where it went wrong and why the police finally caught him. He will change his Modus Operandi and he will refine it. His signature will never change because a Signature is linked to feelings, where a Modus Operandi is linked to rational thinking. One can control and adapt his rational thinking, but changing a long lasting feeling is very hard to do. Most of the Signatures in crime scenes are based on anger, rage, and frustration, the need to humiliate. There are fewer Signatures than there is Modus Operandi.

PART III

Case Studies

CHAPTER 1

Janet

20 December 1989

Christmas holidays have just started. Delphine, a happy little girl is very popular at school. Her best friend is ill in bed. Another classmate invites her to come to her home to play. Delphine is twelve. She is allowed to go alone to her friend's at three in the afternoon. She has to be home at seven, in time for evening dinner with her brother and her mother. Delphine never came home again.

There is no doubt that Delphine and her friend Amy, were together the whole afternoon and that Delphine left some minutes before seven o'clock. It is only two hundred meters from her home along a very busy and well lit avenue. There are a lot of people still around buying their Christmas presents. Shopkeepers are closing their shops and dismantling their display stands outside on the street. That evening several people are also distributing the telephone directories for the New Year. They go from house to house. Somebody leaves the shop with flowers, in front of the cemetery where

Delphine has to walk to her home. Cars are racing by. Nobody saw the little girl. The child seems to have vanished. No fight, no screaming, no suspect moves, no clue . . .

Eight in the evening, the mother of the child starts wondering where her little girl is. She puts on her coat and walks to the house of the girlfriend. She thinks that Delphine must have forgotten the time. She isn't really worried, but unconsciously feels that something is wrong because Delphine is always precise. One can count on that girl. Although her daughter is already very independent and mature for her age, she isn't the kind of girl to leave on an adventure. She is way too young for that.

Christine rings the bell and hears that her daughter left over an hour ago. Immediately she realizes that something is very wrong. In a panic she runs home. She hopes Delphine took another way and they just missed each other. She is hoping against all reason. Her instinct tells her that this is not so. This is the shortest way and the most secure way to come home. There is no reason for Delphine to take another way on this cold, dark winter evening.

The child isn't home. Christine grabs the telephone and starts calling all her friends. She breaks out in a cold sweat and drops the phone several times. While she is calling one person, she already wants to call another one. Nobody has seen Delphine that afternoon. She did visit her sick friend that afternoon, but then she left to go and play with the other one. After that her sick friend hadn't seen her since. Her only hope is that this is just a nightmare from which she will soon awaken. This hope keeps Christine going. She calls her ex husband. Maybe he picked Delphine up and forgot to tell her. He hasn't seen the child either. Her heart beats in her throat and her head, her hands are shaking. She tries to control herself and not give in to panic. There must be a reasonable explanation for the disappearance of her child. Again her fingers slip over the keypad of her telephone. Now she calls all her own friends. Please help me search! She also calls the police, but they say it is too soon to begin a search, they don't seem too concerned.

Friends arrive in their cars and spread out to start the search. They search the whole neighborhood, but there is no trace of the child. The night falls. Christine calls all hospitals in the area. She drives like a mad woman to the police station, because she is not allowed to make a request by the phone.

She has to come to the office. This whole night which seems never ending, all her friends and acquaintances are looking and searching.

The next morning they knock on every door in the area to ask if anybody saw the little girl. Christine is shocked to find that the world doesn't stop turning. Everything goes on in its normal way. People go to work, shops open as usual, buses drive by . . . She is overwhelmed by fear. Delphine is not in a hospital, not with friends or family. Nobody has seen her. There is only one explanation left, but she refuses to even think about this. Not HER child, that is impossible. This only happens to other people's children. People who don't watch their children well. People living in dangerous and dirty neighborhoods. Poor people or isolated families whose children play on the streets all day. Her child is not like that and she herself is not like that either, so it is impossible. It cannot be! A pervert cannot take her child. Never!!

That day passes by, and the next, and the next. The police searched the area, questioned people, reopened files to see if one or another paedosexual could be held responsible for this disappearance. The parents of Delphine are also questioned for many long hours. Days become weeks. Weeks become months.

The general attention for the disappearance of Delphine fades away. People have so many other urgent things to do and anyway there is no trail that can be followed by the police. The mother will be forced to live her life with that loss.

Weeks become months. Like a robot, Christine, starts her job as a teacher again. Nothing interests her anymore. She has become a shadow of her former self. It feels as if a big part of her body has been cut out. She only has her son to live for. The boy has no place in this whole drama. Everything revolves around the disappearance of his little sister.

Some months later the school bag of Delphine is found in a ditch. Her identity card is still in it. Christine doesn't get the information from the police. She heard it by coincidence. A boy waits for her at the school gate, and tells her the news and she starts to cry. He says that the police told him to not talk about this to anybody. Christine is stunned. From that moment she starts to doubt. There is more strange information reaching her. That particular day her daughter disappeared; a car was parked near her house. It was in front of the church with the four doors open. Four men were waiting beside the car. People who left church also saw that event. They had seen that same green Mercedes. Some weeks later a witness sees that car again. He recognizes it because it is a special model and the door is damaged. He notes the license plate and hands the information over to Christine and to the police. The police do not contact her about this. Only months later Christine hears that a woman came to the police station and declared that she was waiting at a traffic light when a car stopped next to her. It was around 7 o'clock in the evening. There was a little blond girl in the back of the car. It was only about hundreds meters from where the little girl left her friend's home. The description of the girl in the back of that car fitted the description of Delphine. The girl cried. The witness was very formal, especially because she remembered having waved to the child to attract her attention. But the child stared blindly with tears streaming from her eyes. The woman gave the description of the driver of the car. She said she was prepared to undergo hypnosis to try to remember the license plate number. The police noted her statement, but apparently nothing happened with this information.

A television station was prepared to release a reconstruction of the facts. No reactions were noted afterwards. A lawyer offered his services free. Later Christine found out that all her personal investigation notes had disappeared. The lawyer claims he never received documents from Christine. A detective came out of the blue to help Christine. He drags her into his adventures and against every deontological code he starts an intimate relationship with her. He abuses her despair and her lonely battle. She is an easy prey to seduce. Christine feels abused, but she would do everything to find her child.

Her financial budget decreases dramatically when a detective takes her with him to Tenerife. Delphine seems to have been seen in a child prostitution network in Tenerife. They try to infiltrate it without success. Christine comes home exhausted.

One day, volunteers propose to sell pictures of children who have disappeared to raise money for the new association Christine founded. Because there is no alternative – she gets no governmental financial aid – she agrees. The volunteers sell over 175.000 Euros worth of pictures. As soon as they have the money . . . they disappear with it. A procedure is pending to bring them to court.

Four years go by. Christine is sitting on her sofa when her ex-husband calls her. He is completely upset: "Christine! Put your television on! Delphine is on the screen!" She throws her phone down and runs to her television. When she finally finds the French program he referred to, the blood drains from her face. Her child is filling the whole screen and looks at her. She doesn't believe what she sees. She doesn't know what the program is about. It is a picture of her daughter and it is in a bad shape. The disappointments she had the last years have armed her. Skeptical she stares at the photo. A woman in the program seems to want to know who this child is. She found her picture a few years ago in her hotel room in Hong-Kong. It was folded in four and put in her belt by someone. That is why it was damaged. The woman has no idea who the child is and thinks that someone might recognize it. Did one of the hotel domestics try to alert her in her hotel for some reason? Is this a bad joke? Many people in Belgium saw the program and phoned the police. The father of Delphine is also convinced that this is his little daughter. Again there is hope. Maybe the child is still alive. Christine calls the French television station. The whole process starts all over again: she talks to the woman from the program but she stays skeptical. She cannot and doesn't want to believe anymore. When she dares to hope, that hope is knocked out of her very quickly and she has to protect herself against new disappointments. She just cannot stand it anymore.

A man calls her from the South of France to tell her that the picture on the screen is that of his own daughter. He sells wallets and had put the picture of his own daughter as a model in the plastic part of the wallets. End of story again.

After seven years almost no one is still searching for the child. Unfortunately there are people trying to abuse the drama. Christine is again dragged into that reality when the media call to tell her that an unknown person received over sixty anonymous letters wherein the name of the killer of Delphine is mentioned. Even Christine's neighbors received such a letter. The man indicated in the letter had been questioned by the police, but had nothing to do with this case. However, again and again the wounds are opened.

One day I asked Christine how she was able to live in that hell all these years. She answered coldly: "It is a nightmare that started seven years ago. I think that I will wake up one day and everything will be over. Then I will hear Delphine in her bedroom and I will hear her coming down the stairs singing. She will give me a big kiss and sit in front of me and we'll have breakfast together. We'll talk a bit and then she will go off to school, as if nothing had ever happened." For Christine this is the only way to deal with this horror. Without that dream, life has no sense anymore.

The most painful part is that Christine stays a main suspect for the police. At a certain point they even considered in digging up her kitchen floor to see if she had buried Delphine under her kitchen. She has been followed, her phone tapped. They kept a permanent eye on her.

Her reactions are not surprising: "For a mother this is unthinkable. Not only do you have to deal with the unbearable fear for your child, you also have to defend yourself against accusations. Added to this that you are at no point involved in the investigations and you don't know anything of what they are doing. You have to read it in the papers the same as everybody else. I cannot describe it. I fought like a lion the last years, but nothing helped. You just cannot force that authority to offer professional help, let alone to build a good centre for victim aid. You are nowhere and you are very lonely in all this. I hope and keep hoping that I can embrace my little Delphine one day. That is all I can do."

Seven years of speculations, rumors and questions

It is evident that in cases of child disappearances one must keep all options open. But in this sad case many very different speculations made it all very complicated. We'll make an overview:

Immediately after her disappearance, the authorities suggested that Delphine was a run-away child. As if a child of twelve years old would organize and plan all this without ever speaking about it to her friends and without having sent out signals that something was wrong. If Delphine's profile could show an introverted child with no friends, a quite little girl, afraid to talk to others . . . then there could have been a slight possibility. But Delphine was nothing like that. She was very social, clever and wide awake for her age.

A few months later the police assumed that an unknown person had taken the little girl that she was murdered and buried somewhere. This was like looking for a needle in a haystack. So they didn't look.

The rumors continued: Delphine was still alive and in a child prostitution network. First she was seen in Tenerife, then in Hong-Kong even in Libya and the United Emirates, there are many rumors but no proof whatsoever.
Then the police were convinced that her own mother had killed her. They even said they thought her body was hidden under the kitchen floor.

Other rumors said that someone she knew and who abducted her and killed her to get his revenge on the mother. Another rumor said that an acquaintance of the mother sold the girl to a prostitution network. In the spring of 1995 some people pretended that a man wanted to get his revenge on all women and therefore killed the little girl.

Let us analyze the facts and the elements.

When we make a profile of Delphine we can see a very independent young girl, but not an adventurous type of girl that would go off alone to explore the world. She adored laughing and the other kids loved her. She wasn't really the great student of her class, but with some efforts she managed to get good results at school. She never played in the streets and was very obedient at home. There were no tensions at home. Just before her disappearance there were no traumatic events like for instance: the death of a beloved one, or a painful divorce or another traumatic situation. We also know that Delphine was not 'the victim kind of girl'.

When we examine the disappearance we can assume that Delphine ran home that night and did not 'walk' home. It was cold that day in December and it rained. Besides, Delphine told her mother some days before she disappeared that she didn't feel safe. She had the feeling that someone followed her. She only had 200 meters to walk to be home safely and so she would only be walking for some minutes. From the standpoint of a criminal, not only the time is very short but also the risk of being seen and apprehended was tremendous: a lot of people in the street, a lot of car traffic and a high risk that the child would scream for help.

Let's assume that the criminal was not unknown to the victim. The child runs home and the offender waits for her in a corner. He talked to her and asked her an simple question or wanted an explanation. In that case he succeeded in making her stop and and listen, he was then able to control her. He convinced her to come with him. The criminal then knows that he has to make the time that he spends with her as short as possible. He cannot show himself in public for a long period of time. An unknown car, parked in the neighborhood could attract the attention of witnesses and somebody might see the child get into the car. Delphine wore a very striking coat in bright pink. If the girl has been taken that way, there has been no planning.

Paedosexuals plan their crimes. They don't take the risk to wait in the rain and the cold, hoping that a child walks by. They look for children in places where they can find children and not in the dark near a cemetery. Only 16 % of the sex criminals do not plan their offences. There is a type of child killer that pulls children in a few seconds into a car, but that type is rather exceptional.

This leaves us with the hypothesis that the abductor was a known person to the victim. An accurate profile of the child's character, her environment and the circumstances of the disappearance leaves us with not much doubt that: Delphine is not the kind of child that would follow a complete stranger, unless . . . that stranger knows exactly what to do and what to say to trap the girl. One of the possibilities is that he waited for her and once he sees her, approaches her. He tells her that her mother has had a car accident and he has to take Delphine to the hospital as soon as possible. Every child would lose control of the situation in that case. It only wants one thing: be with mummy. Children should be warned about this kind of ploy. My investigation of fourteen child killers all over Europe showed me that this 'accident-lie' was often used.

The vision of the multiple child killers on this case

John is a suspect in this case of little Delphine. A rogatory commission questioned him on this case. He told me that the policemen were very friendly with him and they believed him when he said he had nothing to do with this case. Another police department that questioned him in the disappearance of little Natalie in 1991, was very rude. They slapped him and pushed him and hurt him badly. John said he had nothing to do with this case either.

He wrote to me that he as an idea of what could have happened, but he cannot write it down on paper. He wants me to come and visit him in prison. His letter makes me angry, but I can understand that he cannot put it on paper. Such a letter could put him under suspicion as a suspect. Who other than the real killer can know what happened to the girl? I am convinced that John can tell me a lot about this kind of case. He knows how sexual criminals think and act. Only he can place himself fully in the brain of a criminal. He has insight into what motive the criminal could have, how he lives, how he thinks and how he planned his awful crime beforehand. He can also give me a clue of what the criminal did with the body of the child. I am aware that John can tell me a lot about these kinds of crimes: he knows how paedosexual criminals think and act. Only people like him can place themselves fully in the sick brain of the killer. Because they are killers people like John have insight into what motivated the criminal, how he lived, how he thinks and how he planned this awful crime beforehand. He can also give me an idea of where the body of the child can be found.

John's letter gives me to an idea. I ask Christine if I can use some of the letters of her ex-boyfriend. I remembered she didn't know what to think about the sense of those letters he wrote shortly before Delphine disappeared. I remove precisely the data and I change every name in the letters. John will have no idea what those letters are about when he gets them. He will judge them on the sense and on eventually hidden messages I cannot decode. I want him to 'translate' the messages in the letters. From what I send John, he cannot even know it is about the disappearance of a child where he is still the main suspect.

A few days later I receive a heavy envelope. I prepare myself mentally before opening it. One never knows what answers these people like John can send. He can answer your letter in a normal way, he can bury you under a mountain of insults or he can perceive your purpose and give no answer at all. From the title I can already see that John is in a pleasant mood. The letter is overwhelming. Each page is more than fully written. Every sentence has a number. There is structure. Totally concentrated I overview the whole document and while I continue it seems as if John is crashing sharp narrow, little lines in my eye lens. I'm stunned while I stare at the letter!. Everything seems so logical. I take Christine's documents and compare it with the letter of John. Sentence by sentence I analyse the document as well as the interpretation John gives to it. He concludes in his letter as followed: "I hope you now understand. What I wrote are only some ideas about the facts and you can do whatever you want to do with it. But I'm convinced about one thing: the man (ex-boyfriend of Christine) who wrote this letter to the woman (Christine) is very dangerous. I advise this woman to take her children and to move as soon as possible. I can perfectly understand how this man feels because I felt exactly the same when Michèle left me. Just like him I told everybody that I didn't care, while I was completely destroyed inside. The anger of this man is almost touchable in his writings. Can you really not understand what he is planning to do? Don't you really see it?"

No, all this time I really didn't see it. That is for sure! Christine's ex-boyfriend's letter was one like so many of the kind. A desperate letter of a deeply hurt man. A man suffering from rejection. A letter full of pain. Everybody can read this between the lines, yes sure. But what I didn't mention was the anger, the deep deep anger, the retaliation feelings, the hate that transpired from the letter. I am not used to these feelings and so I cannot interpret them. John can, but his warning is years too late.

I write John a letter to thank him for his help and I also explain what this is all about. He answers that he is aware of the disappearance of Delphine but that he never made the link to the letter I send him. He also writes that

Christine has no illusions to make: her child is probably dead and she has to live with that knowledge. He writes a little note for Christine. He states that only people that know what suffering means, can love other people that suffer: "Herein we are equal spirits, Christine, we both suffer."

Concerning the criminal who took Delphine, John is much more reluctant: "What do you want? Do you really want me to confirm what I think about all this? Don't you understand what they are going to do with that man when he is arrested? You don't think they are going to treat him well do you?! No, they will kick him and beat him and put him in prison for many, many years. You know, that won't bring little Delphine back. I don't want to help you anymore in this. The whole system is too repressive. I don't want to hear anything about that case again. You trapped me. You tried to make me a betrayer." I tried everything to convince John that this was not true, but he didn't want to listen anymore. He doesn't want to co-operate in betrayal and self betrayal. The man who is guilty of the disappearance of Delphine is his equal, he is one of his. I have no right to ask him to help bring the criminal to the enemy, the justice department. John identifies with the criminal and feels for him. He calls it 'a poor man that has suffered so much under so many rejections by women in his life'. But he also feels sorry for Christine, but, he says, these things happen and there is nothing you can do about it but accept.

I cannot prevent myself from asking John if this man could still be a danger to other children. He doesn't want to answer this on paper. If I really want to know, I have to go to the prison for this. I didn't. He does not have to think that I will pander to his commands. He doesn't take into account the fact that I have a family, nor does he know that my life is chaotic with too much work to do. I have already driven three times to visit him, thousands of miles away from my home.

However, I transferred all the elements to the judge. I don't know what will happen next, as usual in these cases.

CHAPTER 2

Emma

The 14th of January 1991

At six o'clock the school bell rings in the primary school in a little French town. Eunice puts her belongings into her brightly colored schoolbag. She leaves the school playground with a group of friends. The weather is dark and wet. The nine-year-old little girl has 700 meters to walk home. Since December she was allowed to walk to school and back instead of being brought in her parent's car. She thinks she is old enough to come home alone, she is not afraid. Her parents decided to give her that little bit of responsibility. Eunice runs to join her friends Pierre, Frederic and Bernard. The three boys are having fun on the way home. She runs by them, turns around the corner and only has hundred meters to go before she's home. She will never arrive.

Around six o'clock Eunice's mother comes home from work. Her husband is preparing dinner in the kitchen. It is a day as every day. At six thirty, the mother starts to be worried because Eunice isn't home yet.

She takes the dog and walks to the school. No trace of her daughter. Back home her husband joins her and they go back out again. No result. Maybe Eunice went visiting a friend? But all the parents they contacted had not seen Eunice. They start calling. Nobody saw little Eunice. Panic leaps into the minds of the parents. At eight thirty they call the police. The police respond immediately. Control posts are installed and a description of Eunice is issued to all police stations immediately: 'Girl, nine years old, round face, dark shiny mid-length hair, brown eyes, blue skirt, red panties, blue turquoise coat, black boots with fur, and a brightly colored schoolbag . . .' Searches are started immediately. The family is questioned, a neighborhood search is started. Volunteers are cooperating with the police department. The canal is systematically dragged. When this has no result, the authorities decide to empty it completely.

Thousands of pictures are displayed all over the country and even abroad. The hunting associations are asked to help search the woods and fields. Thousands of people search for a clue. This systematic search does not help. Not one clue that could lead to Eunice or her abductor.

Eunice's parents have the feeling they have stopped living. The desperate mother is convinced that her little girl has been abducted and sold to child prostitution networks. Rumors were already spreading over the area. Even is this hypothesis is awful to think about, she hangs to the desperate thought, "Anything but not her death!" She refuses to lose all hope and clings to that scenario. After three months and two weeks of investigation this hope is crushed: on Sunday 21st of April 1991 walkers find the dead body of Eunice along a busy road hundreds of miles away from her home. The autopsy doesn't reveal much. She died of strangulation. The precise date of her death cannot be indicated more precisely.

A very motivated judge starts an enquiry with the police department. Never before had such an investigation taken place in France. Based on the American model the judge brings together a team of specialists different in each of their fields. Under his supervision a psychologist, a sexologist, different experts, biologists, doctors and independent specialists of all branches are gathered. And, not unimportantly, the parents of Eunice and their lawyer are part of the team. The case is analyzed by all the members of this team and they come together every fourth night. Why was Eunice murdered? Is this the act of a mentally ill person? Is this a retaliatory crime? Has she witnessed something she was not aware of? And is this the reason why she had to die? The files of tens paedosexuals are brought together and analyzed. Hundreds of people are questioned and questioned again when there is doubt.

The approach and the working method of that judge in the case of little Eunice were very brave. They did not wait for government decisions, but they started their investigations right away.

The murderer.

The investigation team decides to reveal some elements in a television program *Témoin n°1* on the French television. After the program something very unexpected happens. A man, who wants to stay anonymous, starts a correspondence with Patrick Meney, one of the presentators of the program. He writes him long long letters wherein he describes meticulously how he killed Eunice. But he also talks about a lot of other murdered children. He laughs about the incompetence of the justice and police department. With an incredible amount of cynicism he describes what he did to the children before killing them. Sometimes he only 'used' the children and sold them later to German prostitution network. Only once he released a child and to prove that he is not lying he describes the story so that it can be controlled by the authorities. It happened years ago. The particular child is a young woman now. And she confirmed the story of the anonymous writer. This is not the story of a fantasy.

The released girl had also been abducted in a matter of seconds. The police immediately put up barriers to stop the abductor. The criminal describes that not only did he see the barriers; he even drove by them with the abducted child in his car. Nobody stopped him. The little girl sat on the floor of the passenger seat. Once they passed the police barrage, she crawled on the seat and looked through the back window of the car. She looked at the policemen and screamed for her daddy. "She screamed for her dad" wrote the anonymous man "and so I thought that her father was a policeman."

The criminal has even the gall to mention the price paid for little children. He claims the murder of Eunice. He explains how he followed her for three days, after he has been informed by another paedosexual who lived in her village. He saw the beautiful little girl almost every day as she walked to school. The criminal drove hundreds of kilometers to check this information. His adult daughter accompanied him on his hunt and presented herself as a nurse to the targeted victims. She was the one opening the car window while they drove slowly next to a victim and telling a story of the mother of the child being in hospital. She convinced the victim to come with them immediately to the hospital. What child would have refused that?! In one of his letters the criminal says without scruples how he raped his own daughter from when she was a baby.

Then the anonymous letters stopped. For more than a year, a new search for information about the killer of Eunice was asked via the media. Evidently the criminal was watching his favorite program. He felt as if he was the main actor in a movie. Immediately he started writing again.

The abductor of Eunice is one of the few types about whom I have already said something in the Delphine case. It only takes them seconds to pull a child into their cars. With arrogance he says that there is no sense telling your children to never go with a stranger. He IS a total stranger for his victims and nevertheless he succeeds time and time again in taking a victim, and this for more than forty years. He has never been caught and he is proud that he is such a good child hunter. It is almost sure that this criminal is a fetishist and that he keeps trophies of each of his prey to remind him of what he has done. He worships his trophies in a sick way. When he feels the need, he takes one of his toffees in his hand and relives his fantasies and masturbates. One day his fetishes will be found and whether they will be thrown away because nobody will understand what they mean, or thanks to these toffees it will be possible to identify lost victims.

The anonymous writer is not only seriously disturbed, he is a psychopath. He enjoys making people suffer in a sadistic manner. It gives him a sexual gratification to hurt others. His profile also shows clearly a narcistic personality. He is convinced that he is smarter than most people and especially the police and he enjoys harassing them by showing them that on that day, that hour, he drove through their barriers with an abducted child in his car. He possesses several false identity documents of children for in case the police stop him.

In his letter he writes that he practiced for years with his own daughter to develop all the skills necessary to abduct a child. Now he is able to trap a child into his car in matters of seconds. When he has no choice he kicks them in the stomach with his large boots. Very often the little victims wet their pants with fear. The smell of urine in little children's underpants arouses him tremendously. While he rapes them, so he writes, he sniffs at their wet underpants or he puts them in his mouth.

"Men do not know what they miss when they don't try the forbidden fruit for themselves. Children are not that innocent. They are little whores!"

The descriptions of that man are gruesome, disgusting and awful and it is important not to conceal that these kind of people exists and live amongst us. Even they alone have a difficult time keeping their secret. Some need to talk in veiled ways about the crimes they commit because they want to know how people would respond to that, others just love it to share their criminal information to hurt that society that rejects them since they were children themselves, on the cruelest level. This anonymous killer will probably be caught one day. He is so sure of himself that one day he will cross a line and reveal himself without even knowing it. Luckily there is still that judge who continues his investigation to find the killer of Eunice. Some police teams would not take such letters seriously. They would consider the writer as a lunatic. They wouldn't even think about investigating the material. It is very probable that the writer would the stop writing one day.

Most of the killers try to keep themselves informed about the ongoing investigations in their crimes. Do investigators take notice of this? Do they recognize the signals? Unfortunately many still approach the behavior and the motives of the criminal from their point of view or their 'normal' way of thinking, although the crime has been committed by someone with an 'abnormal' mind. Hereby the thinking patterns of both parties run parallel and will never cross each other. Those who work in this field must know that they must be able to move themselves in the thinking patterns of such criminals. But how can we know how the criminal thinks when we don't ask him? Many therapists just let their client talk, they don't ask questions, do not extrapolate, do not challenge the client and really do not hear what the manifest message is, let alone the underlying message. After one hour of consultation a judgment is made: X or Y is a paranoid psychopath with pervert tendencies.

To come to a relatively trustworthy conclusion one needs many hours of consultation. I spend hundreds of hours to get an insight into the distorted personality of John only. These hours of study revealed me a lot about these types of criminals in general.

CHAPTER 3

Victoria

The case of Kate reveals that a lack of logical thinking and insight of professionals can provoke indescribable dramas.

A paedosexual or an accident?

Kate, five years old, is brought into the hospital with vaginal bleeding. She was staying with her grandparents when she fell on the corner of a dressing table in the bathroom. Grandpa brings her as fast as he can to the emergency room in the hospital. For several hours the little girl waits for professional help. Grandpa gets more and more worried and begins to feel angry. Kate is his only grandchild and he wants help as fast as possible. But hours in an emergency room is barely normal. The child is losing blood and getting weaker and paler every minute. The hospital staff reports a nervous and aggressive man in their midst and they also note that he claims to have the right be present at every examination of the child. The suspicion making machine starts to run.

The next morning Kate has urgent surgery. Her healing process is only a matter of days, but it will take two months before she is allowed to leave the hospital.

In the press: "A dramatic case of incest committed by a father on his five-year-old daughter".

The day of Kate's surgery, the hospital staff cross-examined her grandfather. The man didn't know what came over them. He only has one grandchild and he adores the little girl. In a blunt way they told him that the girl was raped. Completely upset the grandparents and the parents seek support from each other.

The child is tested with the classical, but absolutely incomplete methods of a game with anatomical dolls. During a role-play with different dolls Kate names the grandfather the 'witch-grandpa'. For the psychologist on duty that day, this is already enough to think that the grandfather is guilty of incest with his grandchild. I have no idea how the questioning has been carried out. Nowhere in the file that I receive later, is mentioned how they had arrived at the incest-conclusion. After a few weeks suddenly the grandfather is cleared from any charges and the father of the child is now accused. The child's story changes constantly. This is one of the elements that show us that the declarations of the child or what has been mentioned by the professional are not relevant or useable. A child that has effectively been sexually abused never changes its story.

The whole investigation becomes even more chaotic when a statement is made that the child has 'been raped by the penis of a sixteen year old'! In what way does a penis of a sixteen year old differ from another man? It is an enigma to me. Some boys of that age are bigger shaped then men of forty. When this statement is undermined, some of the hospital staff start accusing the father as well as the grandfather of the child to be the rapist: and then there is grandma, what about her? No worry, they find a suitable explanation for her role: grandma is the silent witness and accomplice in the whole incest story that has taken place in the family home!

For two months Kate is held prisoner in the hospital. She is not allowed to go out as long as her mother refuses to make a complaint against her husband. Kate's parents always had a good marriage, but it is under serious pressure. The mother wants her child back home and finally agrees after a while to this blackmail. She makes a complaint against her husband and the psychologist of that particular hospital goes with her to see the police. Kate's father is at work when at ten in the morning a police car stops. As in a police movie, he is handcuffed and in front of the shocked colleagues he is dragged out to the police car. Not only does he lose his job, he loses his child and his wife as well. Not to mention his freedom. Suddenly he is released from prison after eleven months while the trial is prepared, but in the mean time he is not allowed to see his daughter. His marriage is broken. His wife had their second baby while he was in prison. She gave birth to another little girl. The baby died some weeks later from sudden death. Frank never saw his child and was not allowed to go to the funeral. That trial took place five years later and all this time is lost for the father and his daughter.

The lawyer of the father has contacted me. I examine the big file against my client. I can read extremely strange statements in it. At a point they ask the father to make a list of all the male contacts the child had. He gives a list of names and I can read in his file that the conclusions of the professionals was that he tried to blame others for the rape. Not only did the psychiatrists contradict each others' statements but one psychiatrist contradicted his own statements several times in one report. In four paragraphs for instance he writes:

1. "Frank is a paranoid psychopath with pervert tendencies."
2. "I do not find paranoid disorders in that patient."
3. "He is a psychopath with pervert tendencies."
4. "He is a psychopath but he is not a danger to society."

Personally I have never heard of psychopaths not being a danger to society. That is what a psychopath stands for. During trial nobody questioned this cruel unprofessional work.

I have only four days to examine the file and to test the man on paedosexual deviations. For days I do nothing else but analyze and re-analyze the whole file. I make notes and examine the contradictions. I compare their statements with my conclusions and tests I took from Frank. At no time was I allowed to approach the child, nor did other experts.

My tests show that the man has no paedosexual deviations. Based on my study of the file, his body language and the declarations of acquaintances, friends, neighbors, witnesses, family members, I cannot understand how they came to such conclusions with such terrible consequences as result. This is a witch hunt that is unexplainable. I still don't know. I can only guess that right from the start the hospital staff made a big mistake. They maybe tried to hide the fact that the child urgently needed surgery, and because they left her alone on a bed for many hours, attempted to divert the attention from these facts which would mean that the child would never have needed surgery if they had reacted in the right and professional way. It seems that the hospital did not want to take the blame. I have no other explanation for it.

Throughout all these terrible professional mistakes and all the resultant misery Frank continues to believe in the Justice system.

Eventually the court was able to divide the truth from the lies and the father has been freed from all blame and accusations. Only now he can start thinking of his future again.

This kind of professional mistake is rather seldom, but I want to warn for the 'ripple effect' of amateurish investigation. Being alert for child abuse and child maltreatment is very important, but I hear different 'clean' people complain that they had very strange questions asked when they presented themselves with their wounded child at a hospital. This is a dangerous situation because it is possible that people start to be afraid to go to the hospital in cases of emergency.

What about Kate? A member of the police department did the interview of the child. He gained her trust and was able to convince her to tell what really happened. She told him not only about her fall in the bathroom, she also told the policeman that some members of the hospital staff made her say things about her daddy that were not true. She also said that these same people changed her statements and told things she had never said.

CHAPTER 4

Evelyn and Peter, Victims of a paedosexual crime?

January 1994

    Christmas and New Year with all its festivities is over. Still in the atmosphere of presents, holiday and staying with friends, ten year old Evelyn and her little brother Peter of seven ask their mother if they can stay over another night with their friends. In the evening that friend would go to his football game and they would join him. Nora, their mother, agrees as long as the children do not go out alone at night. It is cold and wet that evening when the children ring the bell at the door of their friend. His mother says that her son has already left and that she prefers them not to stay over for another night because they stayed the night before and made too much noise. Evelyn and Peter do not make the effort to tell their mum and they decide to go on their own to the football field to see their friend. They take the tram a few meters from their home. Their uncle Bert sees them across the street and he asks them if their mother knows where they are going.

Evelyn says that mum knows and that it is ok. Uncle Bert sees them enter the tram station.

The next morning a little after ten o'clock, Nora wonders where her children are because they promised to be back at ten.

Somebody has to run errands and Nora cannot leave the baby alone. She runs to the friend's house and rings. He opens the door and says he didn't see the children. No, they didn't stay for the night and no he did not see them on the football field.

Nora is in a complete panic and runs to the nearby phone box. She calls a friend. He has a car and he comes to help her search. Nora realises that she doesn't know where to start the search. Where in hell can they be? Intuitively she feels that something really bad has happened. They drive through the city hoping to find a clue to start the real search. But there is nothing. Nothing! At the end of their tether they drive to the police station to report the disappearance of her children. The police say that it is the Christmas holiday and that the children possibly on an adventure. "School starts again on Monday and they will be at your front door in no time."

"But how will they feed themselves?" Nora is desperate.

"Don't worry; they'll feed themselves with vegetables from the fields." A police officer tells the mother. The children disappeared a Tuesday evening. This means that the mother had to wait for almost a week for her two little children to come home, without somebody looking for them. And where in hell could they find vegetables? Antwerp is a big city. There are no fields in that city! She decides not to leave it like this and she contacts the media. She asks for volunteers to help her search for her children. The justice department isn't very happy with that initiative. In fact they are outraged.

Soon hundreds of volunteers present their help and different searches are organized. Finally the police see no other way than to help coordinate the search for the children. Days pass by, there is no clue. The press articles lead to some witnesses who saw the children on the way to the football field. One witness is convinced: the children asked him the right way to the field. He remembered looking to his wristwatch and it was half past seven that night. His wife, who was with him, confirms this. She is sure of the time because she had to feed her baby at half past seven and they were late and in a hurry. They are both the last trustworthy witnesses.

Nora knocks on every door to get help. She participates on television shows and makes several appeals for witnesses to come forward. She writes letters to newspapers. Several reactions followed. Not only from Belgium, but also from the Netherlands where several people claim to have seen the children all over the country. The police are angry and say that the mother is 'media sick'. But on the other hand, some newspapers take the side of the authorities: "These children must be very clever to stay that long out of the hands of the police . . ."

Nora is convinced that something very bad has happened. She also knows that her children didn't run away from home. There was not one reason for them to do that. Peter has poor health and he is very dependent on his mother. She tries to convince the police that her children did not run away, but they don't believe her.

Days become weeks and with such an approach the criminal gets a incredible advance on the police. It is even very probable that he engages in the searches to get himself informed about the scale of the investigation. The participants of the searches are not checked. Much later, an association will check who is taking part in the searches but unfortunately the police do nothing with this information either.

Almost six weeks have passed by. Nora heard on the radio that the body of a little girl has been found in the docks. Her fear is indescribable. Instinctively she knows that it is one of her children. Two days after they had disappeared she felt that Evelyn was dead, but she was also convinced that little Peter was still alive. Her remarks have never been taken serious.

A friend brings Nora to the docks where indeed her child was found, but there nobody can officially inform her of anything whatsoever. The child has to be identified first. A police officer shows Nora a little ring and an earring. She recognizes it immediately and has a nervous breakdown.

Witch hunting or investigation?

The judge contacts me to make a profile of the murderer. The first days the cooperation with the justice department is rather stiff, but still there is some notable cooperation. As a woman one is not easily allowed in this bastion of men. I try to show understanding and patience and I also try to gather as much information as I need to do my job well. I have no complaint about the cooperation with the juvenile police department. We work well together. The police officers are motivated and friendly. I never heard denigrating remarks from them concerning the parents of the little girl. With the Judicial Police department it is a different story, they are awful to work with. Cooperating is almost impossible. I hear nothing but denigrating comments about the parents, but this is not useful information for me. The only file I have is what they compiled before the child was found. It is a very thin file. After the discovery of the body, this department refuses to give me any information at all. At that moment I had never seen the parents, except on television.

Not only do I analyze the file, I also make an appointment with the parents to make a character profile of their child. It is very important for me to make a picture about the children to see if they are high-risk victims or low-risk victims. A victim always plays a role in its own drama. Of course it is not a role the victim chooses to play. It is the killer that chooses the role. He and only he is responsible for what happened. The killer chooses. The victim has been chosen. It is a big difference.

I spend hours talking to the mother to get a clear profile of Evelyn. I note meticulously every answer to my questions concerning Evelyn's reaction in certain situations. Bit by bit I get to know the child. At school she was a very lively and she was able to disrupt the whole class. A little bit mature for her age and a little rebel. Evelyn was impulsive and she often trusted other people too easily She was a young girl full of ideals and she stood for equality and against racism. She adored her little brother and she would die for him. For Evelyn life was a big pie wherein she put her teeth in to eat big parts. In her room, still the same as before she disappeared, I saw lots of furry animals on her bed. The walls were decorated with posters of her idols. On her desk lay her schoolbooks. Her room is a little in disorder as most teenagers' rooms are, but otherwise it is fresh, funny and cozy.

Unfortunately a lot of elements are missing to allow me to work in an efficient way. Not only is there a lot of ill will from the investigation cell, I also see that important information has not been added to the file. For instance, the police do not take into account certain elements that seem of no importance for someone investigating a 'simple' crime, but for me these elements are very very important to refine my profile, because these elements give me an idea of how the killer thought and acted before, during and after his crime. The importance of these elements is totally ignored and I asked several question in this department but they don't answer my requests. I also drive hundreds of miles to look for the pieces of the file myself, but I feel they keep me at a distance from the moment I enter the office. It is obvious that these people have never even heard of a professional investigation.

The lack of motivation and interest of some of these policemen is getting on my nerves. I sometimes get desperate. We are talking about the murder of a little girl and the disappearance of her eight year old little brother! A double murder of two children is extremely rare in Europe. A double crime concerning two children from the same family is even more exceptional.

There is a lot that does not please me. Some people have suggested that I keep on the right side of certain people, and that it would be a good idea to take up a position against the mother of the children. I refuse pertinently. The desperate mother would move heaven and earth for her children. The small talk against her is beginning to undermine the investigation of policemen who at first were very motivated. I am stunned at the effect the small talk has on the investigation. It leads so many professionals away from the issue they are paid for, from the real core of the investigation. It is true that Nora is not a rich woman. It is true that she got married three times and that she has children of three men. It is true that she has no money for a car and a telephone. It is true that her children sometimes played in the streets of the city. All this is true, but in the mean time the strength of the investigation is seriously damaged. From the start there are important leaks to the press.

The media publishes the opinion of some policemen without revealing their identity. 'Name and address known by the newspaper'.

The media reports that the parents are marginal and that they left their children on their own without supervision. Nora sees herself more and more isolated. Nobody wants to be seen with her. Brainwashed by all this untrustworthy and unfounded information, the investigation team feels good. They 'cleaned the house'. The more I refute this situation, the more I get isolated myself. If I am forced openly to take a position: for the police department against the mother or for the mother against the police department . . . my choice is quickly made. Against all their 'reasonability', against every form of opportunism I choose unconditionally for the mother.

My point of view in this is that the team should work together with the parents against the criminal. I'm not heard. For weeks I can only work in fragments. Working in these conditions makes it almost impossible to succeed. With some investigators I have a very good working relationship. They too are disgusted with their colleagues, but are not in a position to complain because their superiors protect some of the 'bad apples'. Those who dare express their opinion and take another position are sanctioned or isolated in the team.

Peter's sweater.

A few days after the body of Evelyn has been found in the dock, a member of the police team finds a little sweater on the spot where Evelyn has been found. He takes it to his office and lets it dry. Although he thinks this has nothing to do with the missing Peter, he wants to show it to the parents. I am present when the parents have to identify several pieces of clothing found in the city. It is the first time I see them together. I observe them keenly while the different pieces pass by. Here and there I see some doubt, but finally they say that nothing seems to be of their children. The policeman carefully brings in the sweater he found. Suddenly all hell breaks loose. Nora starts crying and yelling in panic that this is the sweater of her little boy. There is no doubt: Peter always removed the labels from his t-shirts and sweaters because they scratched his neck. And look, there is no label in it anymore. It has been removed! Completely out of her mind with grief Nora shouts at the policemen that nobody ever believed her when she stated that her children would never run away from home. And the police, because of their indifferent attitude have lost a lot of precious time to find them alive.

It almost ends in a fight between Nora and a specific police officer who had denigrated her and her children from the start. He stands before her with his fists raised and threatens her, but nothing can stop the feeling of outrageous anger in the mother. He grabs her by her shoulders and throws her out in the corridor, where she is 'allowed to ventilate her anger and stop her comedy!'

I am stunned. I leave the office. Nora is sitting on a bench next to a policeman who tries to calm her down. Later I'm informed that they were talking about her demand to see her daughter one last time because she cannot accept or believe that it really is Evelyn they found in the dock. In all our neighboring countries a request like this is accepted. Not in Belgium. Experience showed that parents of murdered children or children, who died in car accidents, cannot possibly start a mourning process when they haven't checked if the dead person is really their child. It helps them to accept that painful reality. Under supervision these parents are allowed to see their children for the last time. In Belgium the prosecutor argues that he wants to protect the mother from more pain. I understand this point of view, but in reality it doesn't work like this. On the contrary, when parents may not see their children, they start imagining the most horrible pictures. Sometimes the body of their child isn't half as badly damaged as they imagine.

After the conversation on the bench in the corridor, Nora's nightmares about her daughter were worse then ever. The head of the police explained her 'emotionally' that her little daughter was not recognizable anymore. They could only identify her on one toe. This idea followed Nora as a ghost. I reassure her that this is a terrible lie and I try to make that image of her daughter more realistic. Evelyn's body was in a very good shape because the temperature under the water didn't rise above 4° C. There was no question of rotting pieces of meat coming off her face and more of these awful stories. I describe again to Nora how her daughter was when they found her. This is against all deontology but I had no choice. I was forced to help Nora out of this terrible nightmare of lies. I explain to her the little details that will convince her that I am telling her the truth. For instance: the little girl still had her chewing gum between her teeth. Her face also showed she has been slammed in her face because there were hematomas on her eyelid. Everything showed that it was a blitz attack and the little girl had no time to react or realize what was going on. The child also looked at peace. This is a totally opposite image of victims that have been tortured to dead. Their faces show fear and terror.

I succeed in convincing Nora that this was not the case with Evelyn. Nora accepts this eventually and comforts herself that maybe her child did not suffer.

Shortly after this event, I receive convocation to come to the office of the head officer. I broke the secret of the investigation, 'secret of the investigation?' And what about the lying details over the body of that little girl? And didn't the policemen break the 'secret' by telling the press and the media details and lies about the family? And isn't it so that the delicate elements of the file that mysteriously ended up in the offices of the newspapers, belong to the investigation?

War went far across the borders of Belgium. Not only did they try to destroy the mother of the girl, even I am under fire now. In this same period of time I was in France for the trial of John. I had to testify as an expert in the case. I presented myself and explained calmly what a paedosexual was and how they can evaluate to child killers. Almost immediately the attorney interrupts me and attacks me on my qualifications. Calmly I explain that I have all my qualifications with me but nobody asked me for them. I asked him to take them and look at them. But he refuses. I am surprised by this reaction, but I continue my explanation. The next day I am confronted with press articles that published terrible lies. "Informed by certain members of the Belgian police department, we declare that this person is not an expert and not a therapist and so is not allowed to make statements on the criminal on trial today." I am stunned again. As usual the source of the lies is not named. I demand correction and I get that easily. But evil has been done.

It is evident that, also for those who seem to be my enemies, I never hurt the investigation especially in such a serious case to which I am very devoted. When I am back in my country, I immediately rush to the office of the head officer in the Evelyn case. I ask him to give me some examples of where I went over the limit. He answers that if he had examples, he would make a verbal protest immediately and he would get me off the case in a second. But he had no examples.

And still the war didn't stop there. At no time have these people been stopped by their superiors, not even when I wrote several letters concerning the incredible misbehavior of some policemen. I never got an answer to my letters either. One day Patsy Sörensen calls me to tell me that three policemen were investigating me. Patsy owns several shelter homes for prostitutes. She has risked her life for many years to help them escape from hell. Patsy is a Europarlementarian now and is one of the most important persons in the world to fight against the trafficking of adult human beings. I treat the childrens' area: disappearances, kidnapping, child abuse, and murder. We have known each other for almost twenty years and she knows me too well to know that I would never do anything to damage an investigation.

Instead of looking for the murderer of Evelyn and the still missing Peter, they were losing precious time investigating me. They warned Patsy that she had to be careful with me because 'I rent children to my paedosexual clients in therapy'. "Join the party!" laughed Patsy: "I threw them out, showed them the door. These same policemen too have damaged her in the past. They mentioned via the media that Patsy saved prostitutes from the mafia, but she made them work for her in a 'closed house'.

If there is a way of damaging an investigation: this is the right way to do it. Only common trust, structural efficiency, professionalism and team spirit guarantee the good cooperation that is needed to resolve such crimes. This investigation is certainly not managed in a structural, human and professional way.

A structured investigation.

The following conditions need to be fulfilled to lead a good investigation.

First every member of the investigation team must have access to all elements of the crime: the pictures of the crime, the file, the autopsy pictures and report, the witness declarations, what has been done so far. Every trace has to be noted in the file. The original file must be sealed and kept safely by those responsible for the investigation team. Copies must be available for the members and they must be able to have access at all times. A conversation with everybody involved the the drama is necessary to be able to draw a profile of the criminal as well as the victim.

A perfect team spirit is absolutely necessary. Clear deals about limits and work methods have to be decided on beforehand to avoid discussions afterwards. Each member of the team has a clear task and discusses his own elements with the other members of the team. Openness is expected from every team member and work has to be done in harmony. On top of this the team must be willing to ask for the help of external experts in certain domains so they can help resolve the crime. Meetings and reunions are needed on a regular basis to evaluate the investigation. Too hasty judgments have to be avoided. Files have to be approached in an objective and neutral point of view.

As soon as the parents are not suspects anymore, it is a plus to invite them to participate in the meetings. Their information is crucial. The parents can imagine how their children would react in certain situations, not the policemen. The investigators did not know the children. Parents know better with whom their children are involved and where there have been conflicts in their lives. This information is very important for the typology of the victims. Are they high-risk victims or low-risk victims?

Starting from the profile of the criminal and the character profile of the victim, a more precise investigation can be directed.

My conclusions about the murder of Evelyn and the disappearance of Peter.

From the character profile of Evelyn I can deduct that she on her own, is a low-risk-victim. By this I mean that there was only a small risk for her to be chosen by a criminal. She was the type of girl that would resist and thus meant a high risk for the offender. He doesn't want to lose a lot of time when he can be seen with the victim. Paedosexual criminals almost always look for weak victims because they cannot afford another frustration. Evelyn was very assertive. She could easily defend her little brother. She was not just hanging around in the city, she had a goal: to see her boyfriend play football.

On the other hand was Peter a high-risk-victim. He was much smaller and thinner then Evelyn. He was easily scared and needed protection. As a child he was often sick and because of the constant sorrow of his mother he was very attached to her. He was not the adventurous type of boy. Rather shy and quite. At school he was hardly noticed by the others. Alone, this child would have been a very easy target for a criminal.

The two children were walking hand in hand beside a very busy road that leads from the Belgian port to the Netherlands. At the side of the road there are only big factories. There are practically no pedestrians. It was very cold, that 4th of January, and it rained. It was also very dark at 7.30 in the evening. And they were walking in the wrong direction. They left the tramway too soon and had another two miles to walk. Instead of taking a right turn, they took the street on their left side. The last known witness said that the children asked him how they could get to the football field. He explained that it was a long way to go for two small children, but they had to go straight on and at the end they should take a right turn at the church. At that point we have to be able to place ourselves in the mind of a child. I walked that road several times and firstly did it through the eyes of the adult. I was wondering why these children did not go to the right as was said, but they took the left side. The third time I did that road I slipped into the brain of an eleven year old. I walked to the church and then looked for the entry of that church. From that point I took to the right as was said and indeed I then ended up in the street to the left because the entrance of the church is behind the building. A child doesn't think the way an adult does. It cannot see the whole picture. So, they probably went first to the church, and instead of going right, they looked for the door of that church which is at the other side. Then they took to the right and ended up in the completely opposite direction of where they had to be.

One witness said to the police that she saw two children walking near the dock. She was not believed because that was not the way they should have taken. This testimony came before Evelyn was found in the dock. The woman was even able to say what the children were wearing. She knew that it was around 7.50pm that night because ten minutes later she was at home when her favorite program started on television at 8.00pm. Her testimony was not withheld. Four weeks later the body of Evelyne was found 50 meters from that place where the children had been seen for the last time.

The twenty minutes between the last witness who explained the way to take and the witness who saw the children walking near the dock are very precise. I did it in fifteen minutes. It is normal that two children took five minutes more over a distance of one kilometer.

Not only did that information fit, the autopsy of her stomach revealed that Evelyn died around eight that evening.

As said, the circumstances play a very important role. The hour and the place of the disappearance almost exclude a paedosexual criminal. These criminals mostly look for children in places where children can be found, and that is not in the dark at night, on a rainy day, amongst a very busy street where the risk of being seen is tremendously high. Weather circumstances do not always play a role, but the chances that a paedosexual goes on a hunting trip on a rainy, wet and dark evening is very small. In such weather he will not have much chance to find a child alone. He hunts near swimming pools, sports centers, schools . . .

Based on all the information I have and the fact that these children were together and not alone, I have to conclude that the whole situation is a low-risk-situation for the children. When we accept that it is a paedosexual crime, the criminal took tremendous risks.

In this case we can almost say for sure that Evelyn and Peter knew their attacker. If an unknown man has to convince a child to follow him, he would have lost a lot of time. Every criminal is aware of this. These kind of criminals are so loaded with frustrations that they will seek an easy target they can easily isolate. As we saw earlier they go through different stages before the eventual attack. There is of course the type of criminal that goes from one stage to the other in matters of seconds, but they are very rare. Normally it takes some days or weeks before they are in the right mood to commit their crime. His behavior would have been noticed by his acquaintances. But it is evident that when the police department waits six weeks to start their investigation, the criminal had enough time to erase important traces.

When a paedosexual crime is excluded, there are other possibilities: a pure rape-case, a psychopath or revenge.

The killer stays around.

From the start I warned the police that this kind of criminal would follow the investigation from a distance.

In one way or another he would try to stay in contact with the family of the children. What I suspected became true, but still the police didn't take notice of my remarks.

In an unimaginable cruel way the criminal contacts Nora. He leaves messages on her answering machine, some months later he enters her apartment building and leaves two strange coats on her doorstep and he steals one coat hanging in the corridor of Nora's house. Nora is in panic when she calls the police, but they simply note: robbery, on their papers.

Nothing else is done about it.

Nora puts little fur bears near the place where her daughter's body has been found. She puts little personal notes for her daughter between the ribbon round the bear's neck. The unknown person takes the letters away and even shows his anger when he doesn't like the content of the little letters. In every possible symbolic way he wants to hurt Nora: he destroys the little cross Nora put near the dock and he puts a white bird whose neck he had broken near the cross. Sometimes he puts several symbolic things together exactly on the spot where Evelyn's body had lain. On Nora's birthday, more then a year after the disappearance of her children, the criminal leaves Peter's football gloves in her mailbox. Peter wore those gloves the day he disappeared. Nora moved after the drama and only a few people knew where she lived. She reported this to the police. A few weeks later she asked the police if they found anything on the gloves. She gets one reaction: 'Do you really think it is that important?"

At the end of the rope.

A year after the crime, Nora tries to end at her life. She survives, just. In a letter she begs me to help her. She is on her own, with her remaining child, Axel, who is two years old. He has terrible nightmares and he lacks sleep. She cannot bare this situation any longer. She cannot live with the pain and wants to put an end to it. For months I don't hear anything about the investigation, while the criminal continues to harass her. Her life has become a living hell and nobody does anything to stop it. I realize that, when Nora isn't there anymore, the whole investigation will grind to a halt and a very dangerous criminal stays free, unpunished. Who will continue to harass the police if she isn't there anymore? The children's grandparents are also at the end of their tether. Not only do they have to live with the drama and the knowledge that their little grandson is still missing, they also have to be there for their daughter to support and comfort her in her immeasurable grief. These people don't know what to do anymore. I ring the alarm bell several times. The authorities do not react. Not once.

I have only one solution left. While I'm not in favor of contacting the media, the fourth power in Belgium, I convince myself that I have no other choice. Otherwise Nora is going to die. She would be another victim, not only of the killer of her child, but also of a completely incompetent police system. I had already been contacted eight months after the facts by a journalist of a very famous magazine, but at the time I refused to reveal elements of the investigation. He also wanted to know my opinion about the mother of the missing children. I answered him that I was totally alone in my belief that this woman was absolutely normal. He then contacted the mother to make his own objective opinion and also concluded that Nora was a normal, intelligent and emotional woman, not at all the image that was drawn of her by the media. He asked me to work with him on an article about the true Nora. But because the investigation was still ongoing and I was afraid to damage it, I thought it was not the right moment to do so. I was aware of the consequences of my comments on the investigation.

Months later, when the impasse was complete, I reconsidered my decision. I also realize that this situation could have dangerous consequences for other children. A man, able to abduct two children and kill one, will stay quiet for a long time. I feel in conflict: on the one hand, the investigation is literally 'pending', on the other hand I would never forgive myself if another child is killed without me having done everything in my power to prevent this. The same journalist contacts me again: I know what to do and agree to reveal the whole disgusting 'investigation' publicly. Nora has already agreed to talk to him but she is afraid that her cry in the dark will not be heard without serious back-up. I decide to give her that back-up. And because I never hide behind anonymity, I speak freely under my own name.

Two days after the article is published, a little boy is found in a ditch. His body had been there for at least three days. A heavy silence is surrounds the case. In the press there is a short article claiming that it is not little Peter and that the victim had committed suicide. Nothing more!

In the mean time I wait for the eventual sanctions concerning my intervention in the media about the case of Peter and Evelyn. But time goes by and it becomes more obvious that the police want a cover-up and forget the whole case. All of a sudden, without a notice, I am convoked by the authorities to explain my point of view. No telephone call, no letter… nothing. A police officer told me that they will have an internal investigation. Strange! Only Nora and I talked about the very unprofessional working methods of that police team and neither of us is invited to explain whatsoever in the 'internal investigation'. How on earth will they investigate what is going on? We didn't mention the names of the incompetent police officers in the article. Why have we not been invited? Not reacting, keeping complete silence is a way to kill an investigation too. It is a very good strategy. A few days of 'fuss' and afterwards everybody has forgotten about it. The mother has nothing else to do than to try to forget that she once had three children.

Balance

Almost two years have passed after the murder. Nothing has been resolved. There has been a lot of work done, but in such a chaotic way! Investigators were falling over each other, people that wanted to work in a structured way were hindered by those thinking they knew better. Just because a file is one metre high it does not mean that an adequate job has been done.

The biggest mistake was made right at the beginning: they didn't take Nora seriously about the disappearance of her two young children. Even if they had run away from home, they would still have been in great danger. The chances of them falling into the wrong hands in a city such Antwerp, is very real. In those circumstances the authorities have to react instantly. One cannot afford to 'wait and see' what happens. The killer had exactly six weeks ahead of the authorities. The bad weather had erased traces, evidence had been lost by the police and some witnesses weren't taken seriously, let alone investigated.

When the body of Evelyn was finally found, the fire brigade put her body on the side and cleaned her face to try to identify her. Such a 'cleaning' should not have been done. Firstly the forensic team has to take all the samples of all traces and evidence. Perfect pictures have to been taken of the position of the body before anybody touched it. As a result a lot of evidence was lost.

In the case of one child being found murdered and the other is child still missing, the file is handed over to two services. These services lie kilometers away from each other. Not only does the distance make good cooperation very difficult, but also the fact that those services come under different authorities doesn't make it any easier. The youth department depends on the mayor of the city. The Justice Police depends on the Ministry of Justice. Each service has its own way of working. This should not be a problem, on the contrary, both services could work perfectly together if there is good cooperation. But that is not the case here. It is strange that the file was not sent to the murder department, but it continued to circulate in the Youth department.

It is evident that the investigation starts in the immediate surroundings of the victims. This should take place in the calmest circumstances possible. You need to have an important amount of empathic skills to understand that the parents live in incredible fear and stress. It is not favorable to harass them even more. In this case the investigators abused in the most gruesome way the feelings and despair of the mother. The most incredible lies were spread about Nora, which had nothing, absolutely nothing to do with the facts. On top of this Nora was not kept informed of the progress of the investigation on her own children. She had to read everything in the newspapers. Not once was she invited in the office of the judge. He didn't know her. Had never seen her and based his opinion on what the investigators told him about her. I often suggested that the judge meet her so he could form his own opinion, but he refused saying that it is up to the parents to contact him. This step is too high to take for people in this situation. But that didn't seem to get through to him. A meeting with the parents of a victim is crucial to understand what happened. It doesn't have to take much time. A short meeting would have convinced the judge that what he had previously heard about them didn't fit the real profile of the parents. He could have re-directed the investigation and very probably there would have been much better results than they had.

Only a few people took their responsibility. They did it on their own initiative. Now and then they informed the parents of what they were doing. One of them called Nora to say that they had found a little boy in the water and that it wasn't her son. He didn't want her to hear it on the radio. I meet some very professional people at the police department too, conscientious and motivated men. Their colleagues don't always appreciate these 'good' examples. They feel threatened. They are isolated and ridiculed, nobody talks to them anymore. They become the victims of intimidations and gossip. The consequences can be disastrous. For instance: the police officer who found Peter's sweater, was isolated immediately. Rumors were spreading that claimed that he could be the killer himself: "because it was unlikely that it was always him who found clues . . .". It is now quite possible that when this police officer finds something again, he will be cautious and will think twice before making another move. If he even plans to do so in the future.

Elements that show these bad investigations are legion: No attention has been paid to the strange 'communication' between Nora and the unknown person who put little notes on the bears near the dock.

When Nora was followed for weeks by an unknown person, she called the police to inform them that she was afraid. The police searched that man and brought him to her apartment for confrontation. He even talked to Nora. Nora would not speak to this man into her flat and the whole conversation took place in the hallway where neighbors could hear what was said.

The coats Nora found in her house were not noted, so it is obvious that no forensic team investigated the evidence on them. I talked to the head of the forensic team and he had never heard about the coats! The information brought to the judge was so deformed that the poor man didn't know what was really going on.

The parents uninformed about their duties, nobody told them what their rights were. They were never told that they need to take a lawyer to defend their rights and to do the follow up of the file. They could have taken a pro-deo lawyer. But nobody told them anything. It took seven months before they had a lawyer. Poor people or badly informed people do not seem to have the right to justice.

On top of this, I find the fact that professionals have spread gossip and lies, this constitutes a very serious professional mistake. We also call it a lack of elementary education. However, the lack of motivation, team spirit, professional skills and professional education and sometimes the lack of financial funds are disastrous ingredients for professional investigations.

While reading the file of Evelyn and Peter, I couldn't ignore the fact that each officer tried to explain the case on his own in order to take the credit. But such serious crimes are almost impossible to solve alone. They cry out for teamwork. In some cases we need to search for unsolved cold cases to be able to compare the information of this case with the new case. Sometimes it is beneficial to request from investigators in other countries about their experiences of similar crimes, because as we have seen before killers don't care about boundaries.

The way most parents of victims were approached in Belgium, France, the Netherlands... by some of the investigators was absolutely inhuman. Things changed a little since the Dutroux case, but it is sad to see that we needed such a drama to be able to be more human with victims and families. In some cases we can speak about 'class justice'. It may sound strange but children from rich families have less chance to be believed when they report child sexual abuse, than children from poor families. Especially when it concerns incest the police are reluctant to believe a child from, for instance, a lawyer or a doctor, than they would believe a child of an electrician.

On the other hand, we can see that everything is done to find a missing child from a rich family while for a child of poor parents they are advised to wait some days and see what happens. A double parent family is thought to be more trustworthy than a single parent when their child is missing. Justice departments never speak in a patronizing manner to high class people as they do with the lower classes. But a child stays a child, no matter from what class it comes. The child is missing and so it is in danger. It is the duty of the authorities to do whatever they can to find it. They are paid for this.

Number 94/44 – classified without result

Because it becomes more difficult to find evidence and witnesses over time, I see myself forced to find other solutions to avoid the fact that also the cases of Evelyn and Peter will be classified with the thousands of other cold cases. I contact the General Chief Constable of the justice departments and I send him a file wherein I explain everything that has gone wrong. Not one reaction. Some weeks later I telephone. His people tell me that I don't have to worry, they guarantee that my file will be transferred to the highest level, but as usual nobody informs anybody. I don't trust the whole thing and I contact the prosecutor concerned and as I suspected he didn't receive anything.

Shortly after this my phone rings. A family member of Nora is on the point of a break-down. He says that the whole investigation has to be done all over again. One of the police officers, who didn't stop spreading rumors about not only the family but also me and his colleagues, stopped the family member in the street. He threatened him saying that the investigation will be done all over again and focused on a 'particular person'. He also 'smoothly' asked if the man in question still had contacts with me. He said no and the gossip started again: "She is dangerous, you have to be careful..."

The real question should be: for whom am I dangerous in fact? Especially for those I nail on the wall because of their misbehavior. I started to question around and heard that indeed the investigation had to be done all over again... with the same investigators. It is, in one word: desperate. The only positive point is that for the moment the file will not be classified without result. I suspect it is only a matter of time.

I know a case of a six year old boy who disappeared in the centre of Brussels many years ago. One officer doesn't let it go. He investigates every little clue he has. Also in other cases individual police officers continue to find clues, but they are rarely supported by their superiors. Maybe it would be a good idea to bring those people together so they could compare their working methods and knowledge.

Victim aid

It is a good thing that there is something as 'victim aid' for parents of murdered and missing children. But it can only help when the file is closed. Nora cannot expect any help from that department and it can take years before she reaches that point. But also in this period of waiting, the need is high to receive some financial help. Nora had to install a telephone for which in fact she had no money. She needed it to be able to call the police, to call friends to help her find her children and also to wait for news of them. Maybe her little boy will find a way to call for help. So Nora distributed posters carrying her telephone number all over the city, hoping that her children would see it one day.

For a short time she received some help from a nongovernmental association, but very soon she was on her own again. As soon as the press published that her children had disappeared she had no right to financial child care anymore. Not one sign of humanity and no questions about her life circumstances. They just discontinued her financial help. The least a governmental association could have done would have been to contact the parents themselves and ask them what their needs were in this tremendous burden of paperwork and administration of bureaucracy.

Parents can not possible concentrate on such things. They don't have that time because they have to be permanently present for the justice departments, the police, the media . . . They also have to cope with their despair, their grief, their panic. Why doesn't the association take the initiative and to come to the aid of these parents?

In this field of help for victims our society still has a lot to learn. For instance, Nora should have been able to count on a psychologist for help with her grief and fear. But he decided when Nora could come to talk about her grief. As if the feelings linked to very traumatic events can be controlled so that it can fit into the working hours of the caretaker. There should be a permanent help line for these victims. People suffering from such trauma must be able in every circumstance to call somebody when it becomes too much for them. There is not such a service. Some non-governmental associations have to do with what they have, they receive no funds and most of the time they don't have the professional skills to deal with such serious problems. Very often these associations have been founded by families hit with very traumatic events in their lives themselves and every time they hear the story of someone else, they are confronted with their own grief.

Nora is not alone in this situation. Other parents of missing and murdered children when the criminal has not been caught, are in exactly the same situation. Many parents aren't even aware of the possible help they can get. Why don't these organizations make the first move to contact the parents? Why does the first step always have to come from those who suffer? Isn't it the task of the government to care for its citizens?

I want to end this chapter by saying that this lack of help also hits other groups of our society: the homeless, drug addicts, sick people, elderly and other unfortunate people, see how our governments arranges everything but have little attention for the deprivation that strikes many of us.

More and more the initiative has to come from the man in the street. The more people struggle to try to find funds themselves, the more governments conclude they can manage without governmental aid. They abuse the kindness of some of our society who does care about the less fortunate. They are more concerned with such problems as the color of the traffic lights which takes weeks than why a lot of people do not know how to feed their family at the end of the day. Thousands of dollars or Euros are spend on things no one has asked for. Solidarity is pushed more and more in the background. A society where each individual only thinks of his own rights without a thought for others is a sick society. We see more and more that the individual interest comes before the general interest.

Almost everybody is pushed in boxes and isolated and we can barely say that we still live in a 'society'. There are alcoholics, homosexuals, lesbians, disabled, thieves, jobless, paedosexuals, rich, poor, people without talents, green, hormonal, mafia, racists, abused children, neurotics and psychotics, politics and drug addicts, dealers, honest and dishonest, stupid and smart, orphans . . . In which box do you belong? All these aspects make a society what it is. One cannot separate all these groups. Wouldn't it be better to attach every group to the whole of that society, or is the individual right too entrenched into our spirits that we don't even consider this option?

PART IV

Pedosexuality and Society

PART IV

Bisexuality and society

CHAPTER I

John's Story (Part III)

1.000 Letters from hell

Thousand pages of letters from John! Most of the time he tries to minimize the facts. He complains about the way the press talks about him. They try to describe him as bad and disgusting as possibly. He reproaches the media that they exaggerate the facts to 'unbelievable proportions'. He complains that his wife doesn't write to him, that she throws his letters unread in the bin and that his children don't want anything to do with him anymore. He also feels so sad and lonely.

I answer:

"John, what the media writes or says, has no importance. You and only you have to realize what you have done. If you are so convinced that what they write is wrong, why don't you prove the opposite? It is possible that you feel regret for what you have done, but what do you plan to do about this? Waiting for aunty Mine to mend the broken pots? Stop hiding yourself behind a mountain of self pity."

"Every day again, I wait for news about my wife and my children, as I wait for news from you."

"Well, John, every day millions of people in France are waiting for an answer from you. Every day! Every hour the parents of the little victims ask themselves: why?

The world is much bigger than how you see yourself, your wife, your children and me. The world is waiting for a letter, a word, a sign of regret for what you have done. Regret coming from your heart. Not some rational thought, but sincere regret."

"To your letter I am adding a letter to my wife, despite her silence."

"Silence! ... do you want me to continue Jan? Are you going to continue to hide in your closed world?"

"No, I don't expect forgiveness, because what I did cannot be forgiven. I only expect some understanding. I would like to die. Since this drama I regret every day of what happened. Why am I a paedosexual? I get to the point that I don't know what I did anymore. This illness that continued to grow like a merciless machine, an endless turning and growing wheel since my youth, a movement that I had to stop at any price. Maybe I wanted to kill the paedosexual in me by killing those children. Maybe I wanted to stop this hellish machine from turning. I don't know anymore. I will try to explain to you how I felt in the year of the drama. I had felt bad for so long. I wasn't really angry, it just didn't work. Let's say that it was slightly raining inside of me. During the summer of that year, a storm developed in me, and shortly after a real tornado was hitting me. Incredibly fast this storm changed to a hurricane that pulled everything with it on its destructive way. At the end of 1991 there was this apocalypse and I stood in the middle of it. Eye to eye with those two children, a strange feeling of calm overwhelmed me and it was clear to me that I found myself in the centre of the cyclone. I felt an enormous pressure in my ears. The silence was deafening. Nothing moved at the moment of the drama. For me the fatal moment arrived and there was no way for me to avoid it. This must be the end of my paedosexual behavior. At last I would be free! Not one moment I thought about those children. Not one moment.

Immediately after the deed I felt myself pulled out of the eye of the cyclone and I was again dragged in this howling wind. I rushed to Lourdes to seek help, but the Holy Mary was outraged with me and closed the gates right in my face. I couldn't get in. This diabolical wind dragged me to a hotel where I tried to put an end to my miserable life. It isn't easy to put all this into words. I didn't feel outraged at the others, but more at myself because I was unable to put my life back together.

Only many months later I realized that those children had parents, parents who were dying from grief and anger. As for me . . . they weren't even children. They were objects as I have always been one. Objects have no feelings, so you cannot hurt them.

Weeks before the drama I felt a very deep grief inside of me. I didn't know why. I felt that something was going to happen but I didn't know what. I thought about my own death. I was unable to make my feelings clear to anyone, because I couldn't even describe for myself just what it was I felt.

You can compare it to someone who is standing in a storm. He is yelling something to his neighbor, but the neighbor doesn't hear it. I lost my job, my dignity, my family, my house, my weekly appointments with my psychiatrist and I had no hope for my future anymore. Maybe you can understand now what I am trying to explain about that 'storm'.

The destabilization process started with the break up with Michèle in the United States. I never got over this. I cried in the arms of Anne. My psychiatrist told me he couldn't help me. I was chased out of my house in which I had worked so hard, I was banned from my village like a dog completely left to my own. Me, that never learned to take care of myself! Shortly after this the drama happened.

Many times I have wanted to write to the parents of the girls, but what do I say? I'm sorry? It will never happen again? This is ridiculous! Such a crime cannot be forgiven. And even if I could try to explain to the parents, this would be in complete contradiction with that what is in the file about me. They wouldn't believe me anyway, and on top of this, it would re-open the wounds, wounds that are healing so slowly.

I realize that now, but unfortunately it is much too late.

For me it has always been clear why this drama had to happen. Everybody dropped me, even my doctor and on top of this the most renowned psychiatrist of Paris told me he couldn't help me. So I knew what I had to do. I had to kill the devil inside of me. No psychiatrist believed me when I explained clearly that I had two personalities inside of me and that one of them was the devil himself."

In a frenzy of insanity John asked the parents of the victims how much he has to pay to compensate the damage he inflicted.

I ask: "John, can you imagine this scenario: your little son Cédric disappears from the garden. Describe to me what you feel. Describe to me how you try to calm your wife down and how do you start looking together for your son. How does it feel to finally call the police in complete despair? What is going on inside your head when night is falling and the little boy is still not back? Maybe somebody took him? Hours pass by and your despair is increasing. Anne cries without stopping and you as a father, don't know how to comfort her anymore. You call all the hospitals in the area, but nobody has seen your little boy, John. Maybe he fell into a well and is he crying for your help. You search whole night while Anne is waiting by the telephone. The police are helping and the neighbors and friends unite their forces to help.

You don't know what to say to Anne anymore. There are no words. You are scared to death yourself and you know she will hear it in your voice. Hours pass slowly. After the night, comes another day and then another night again. Days become weeks and weeks become months.

After all this time, nobody is still looking. Everybody has so many other things to do. The world doesn't stop turning, John. Deep in yourself you know that your little Cédric isn't living anymore, but there is that never ending hope that keeps you looking for him. You need to know.

Then one day the police arrest a man. He confesses that he has taken your child, he has sexually molested the boy and finally strangled him. He has thrown the body somewhere in a wood like a garbage bag or a used condom. The murderer of your son says to you: 'I will financially reimburse you for the trouble I caused you by killing your child, how much do I owe you?'

Imagine then, John that you want to ask the murderer: why my child? You write to him in prison. You want to know. Your wife becomes crazy because of the grief and the pain. What would you like him to answer you? Would you, the father of the murdered little boy, be able to understand the killer? Would it suffice that he says: 'I am so sorry.'? Would you prefer he doesn't answer your letters? Wouldn't you have the feeling that he isn't taking your feeling seriously? That he doesn't care how you and your wife feel? Will the memory of your son disappear also?

I think, John, that any communication, however difficult it might be, can help to ease the pain and to canalize it. It is also that you only see what you want to see. You pretend that the two little girls you killed were not afraid. They were. You didn't want to see that they were frightened to death of you. An adult is always an authority for a child. For a big part, those little girls must have felt guilty about the fact that they ignored the rules of their parents to never follow a stranger. You have abused this feeling of guilt in the most shameful way against them. For these children you were not this ugly, old, dirty man. You were nice and friendly, you gave them lemonade in the car and they were allowed to read the books you bought to trap them. You knew how to handle children. In the eyes of children such nice people do not harm them.'

John is outraged. The confrontation with this reality is hard. His anger is visible on the envelope I pick out of my mailbox.

"What do you earn in writing such a story!? Do you think I don't know all of this! You do consider me a monster, thus! just as the press has described me. If I only had thought that those children had parents, none of this would ever have happened . . . but I was thinking nothing at all. Nothing at all!

I am prepared to answer your questions concerning the scenario you force me to imagine. I would like to make a point that I would never ever want to hear anything about the case. I would prefer to kill the murderer of my son, but it is also possible that I would go to prison to meet the murderer to talk to him. I would then like to know if he is accountable for his acts. If that is not the case, I would try to forgive him with God's help. But I would also take care that the man is sent to a mental health hospital. There would not be a way in between. There are no 'in between solutions' in these cases. It is one or or the other. I didn't torture these girls, I swear on everything that is precious to me. All the letters I wrote to you to convince you that I didn't hurt them and now it is clear that it was all for nothing. You wouldn't give me a chance to repair something to the world!!'

John continues to deny reality. I never understood why he does that. The autopsy results are undeniable: the children have been brutally tortured for many hours. There is no other explanation. John has to learn to accept this and live with it.

John writes often and many pages, three times a week sometimes, but he stays very superficial. It is obvious that he is afraid of sanctions because his post is read by the prison personnel. I need to go to his prison to talk to him, more than a thousand kilometers away.

Eye to eye with John

The prison where John is staying is a picturesque building in the mountains. With its white walls and bright red roof it looks more a big farmhouse. Before entering it, I observe it carefully. A camera is watching me. An over three hundreds year's old prison with a camera . . . it seems a bit unreal. I ring the bell and hear the rattling of keys on the other side of the thick door. After filling in the necessary administration I have to go through a detector. The guard takes me to a separate room. John cannot have visitors in the same room as the other prisoners because it would certainly mean his death. It takes a whole organization to foresee a separate chamber.

A few minutes later John enters. It is not a surprise. I already know him. Shaking like an old man he takes his place in front of me at the little table. Our first contact is easy until sudden John goes on the defensive. "As long as I am not convicted I am innocent! I didn't do it!" he yells.

We talked so often about this in our correspondence. I lose my patience and that is due to a serious lack of sleep. John is hiding behind lawyer's talk, while I travelled thousands of kilometers to hear the truth. Only with the truth can I help John out of his hell. After several arguments going back and forth, he now pretends nothing has happened. "There are fifty million French people who could be the killers as well." This is way too far out of line.

"How do you explain the two little bodies?!" I am angry, very angry. "Do they exist or not? Did you show the authorities where they were or not? You told me yourself that you even didn't recognize them when they were brought up. You told me so many details that the authorities aren't even aware of and now you are trying to convince me that nothing ever happened! If you hadn't shown them where the bodies were, they would never have been found. Only the man who did this could know that."

He stares at me with a desperate face. "You want me to be locked up forever. Of all people you abandon me. You absolutely want to hear me say that I did it. You don't believe me, do you. Just as all the others!" He hisses to me.

There is no sense to argue on this because the facts are proven. I didn't travel all that way to have such useless conversations. I want to dig deeper in his swampy brain, I want to scrutinize and understand him to be able to work on prevention with this knowledge. John attacks me, he stamps his feet and cries like an obstinate child that is wrong but doesn't want to admit it. Out of his powerless feeling, he suddenly grabs my hand, immediately he lets loose a little bit while his eyes ask if I am afraid of him. I am not. He lets loose a little bit more, apologizes and asks me to not abandon him. I didn't plan to. With my free hand I take his other hand lying on the table. I show understanding and support for the hell his whole being is living in. John cries. He is confused. This is the first human touch he had in more than two years. No kicks, no hits on his head, no punches in his ribs. For minutes we say nothing. We only look at each other. I don't feel anything. I feel empty inside", you touched me" echoes soundless in the cell, "you touched a monster."

I let the emptiness in me fill up with his despair.

"I know."

My ticking watch in the hollow room is audible while this wordless conversation goes on.

"You can take your hand back, I won't blame you. I will understand."

"Why should I do that, John?"

"Maybe you got dragged along by the situation and now you regret it."

His clammy, cold hand stays lifeless under my warm hand. He dares not move. He dares not break this moment. The situation has become unbearable for him. My face is emotionless. He sounds out every corner of my face, looks penetrative into my eyes, but doesn't find anything. He doesn't know what to do in this situation. Wordlessly this conversation goes on:

"I don't let myself be dragged along in situations, John."

"But I am a monster, a brute. With these hands I killed two little girls!"

"I know."

"You touch these hands now."

"I know."

The silence is oppressive. His hands begin to shake uncontrollably. He bends his head, broken. Outside I hear the rattling keys of the guard again. He approaches with fast steps. He is worried about this long silence. I can see by John's reaction that the guard is looking through the bars to verify that everything is alright. John thinks I will look up, but I don't.

"Everything alright Miss Hutsebaut?" asks the guard.

I answer without looking up: "Everything is alright, sir."

John doesn't understand. He suffers awful pains under my left hand that surpasses the dominant pleasure on my right hand. When the situation has become unbearable, I pull my hand from under his and put it on his shivering hand. The icy silence stays.

He wants to know what I feel and I want to know what he feels. He runs loose in my eyes while I smash myself to death against his. He looks into the world through my eyes and I stand in front of the gates of hell. Behind these gates is John he cannot come out and I cannot get in. There are no pupils in his eyes, no entrance. In front of these gates lays an ocean of tears.

"Let me in, John." I whisper finally.

"I cannot."

Around us everything has become black in a strange and ultimate moment of intimacy. Together we are powerless. There is no world around us anymore. There is nothing, emptiness. A little river of despair flows along us; a small brook of fear is invisible, but ripples audibly. Splinters. Fragments. Our hands bridge an inscrutable stream of grief. Very far away again the sound of keys and feet. Reality returns very suddenly. Bars are opened and John is taken by his shoulders. He stands up slowly while his hands stick to these mysterious moments for a while. The eye contact stays uninterrupted. Slowly I stand up while fixing his eyes. John steps backwards with the hand of the guard on his shoulder. He continues to look at me. The bars open behind him, his hands let loose. John is swallowed by the darkness of the corridors of the prison. For a while I stand there emotionless.

"Miss, visitors' time is over." Mister H. says softly, almost apologetically. He is the under director of this prison and he is a very sweet man. A human being you rarely see in these kind of institutions. He doesn't judge, he leaves that to the judges. He takes his tasks whole heartedly and tries to ease the pain for prisoners by being as humane as possible. They are also human, he says. And he is right. He is a very good man. And therefore he is respected in the prison. Although I normally have a right to half an hour visit, he allows me to stay for three hours. They understand the work I am doing. They leave me alone with John. A guard is around in case of trouble, but he is not visibly present.

I leave the visitors room with an empty feeling inside. While I walk through the space between the cells and the exit, I turn around and look again at the door through which John has disappeared. A cell of two meters by three, home for the rest of his life.

While I wait for the gates, that separate me from freedom to open, I see a room that looks like a fairy tale. The virgin white walls are painted with wild blue seas. Swirly waves rise up and I can almost feel the streaming water on my face. A wonderful beach with beautiful white rearing horses that make me almost move back. Living manes dance around the proud heads and the whirling sand falls down on my feet. In my imagination I trot with the horses, jump over a little barred door and stop before a giant ivy that creeps along the central heating element to the ceiling. A part of the ivy hurls its way via the bars to the entrance hall. On the wall behind me is a century old clock where time stays still as it will for so many here who have left time for always behind them the day they entered.

I experience the freedom that had always been taken for granted and I almost feel guilty about it. I leave this space, awakened again by the clattering keys that open the doors for me.

The prison staff understands my silence. I thank the director and say a friendly: "See you tomorrow."

Now I really am outside. The glittering sun welcomes me. I turn myself to her warmth. Everything shines. Birds are singing their freedom and the mountains look happy. I have to get used to it a little bit. I can put my foot to the right, but I also have the choice to put it to the left. During those few hours in prison I didn't feel this freedom. Now she is back and I enjoy it. I decide to have lunch; I can even choose what I want to eat. Never before was I so aware of these little 'happy making' things. The spaghetti on my plate seems better then ever before. I talk with the other guests, we laugh a bit and later that evening I go for a short walk. At midnight I go to my hotel and I decide not to think too much before going to sleep. After two days without sleep and the very exhausting meeting with John, I fall asleep like a rock.

Iron Lady

The next morning I am back in prison. I give my handbag to the staff, pass through the detector and jump back frightened to death when the alarm signal screams loudly. I empty my pockets, pull hairpins out of my hair and try cautiously to take another step forward. The staff finds it hilarious when the thing spits me out again. I hear someone say 'iron lady'. A guard points at my shoes and indeed there is iron on it. I am allowed to keep my shoes on, barred doors open and close again behind me.

John comes into the visitors' room. The feeling of recognition I had the previous day is gone. He is different. This is not the man I saw yesterday. I have never met this man here. He is aggressive and barks, he cuts as a knife and tries to get me off balance with the most gruesome details of the crime he committed. He talks about masses of blood while he observes how I react and if I lose my balance. I don't give in. Don't feel anything. My suitcase of feelings stays at the prison gate, outside. Otherwise you cannot do this job.

I amaze myself when I hear myself ask ice cold, if he agrees to sitting at the little table. Without preparation I handle him as a bad little boy of six. He isn't much older than six on an emotional level. The whole conversation is aggressive and sharp. It is very exhausting, but it helps me to understand how he functions. Today I get to know the other side of his personality, the side of the man who killed children. The nice, friendly, helpful man his friends know, is only a façade of the other personality. One cannot catch flies with vinegar!

Somewhere in his life his personality got split. It is very probably that this was during his adolescence. The splitting of his personality was the last step in a long process of years. If someone could have reacted in time, while he was still a little boy, it is very probable that John would never have become a killer. If, when seriously damaged and traumatized little boys meet someone that loves them, it helps them. This is someone to whom they can look up, this can be the deciding factor for the rest of their lives. But this helping hand must be there before the end of puberty. When traumatized children find one point of support, even if it is only one, they will probably not have a virgin existence but the chance of them killing someone is much less. After adolescence it is often too late, then for them their parallel world has become a fact. In this world there is no room for love and friendship. There is only room for hate and anger.

CHAPTER 2

Public Opinion and the Media

Violent reactions

When people are confronted with crimes as child rape and child murder they react with outrage, violence and bewilderment. This evil must be revenged. This instinctive reaction is understandable. A law is broken. A law that counts in all societies wherever in the world. It's not just a law. I would call it a natural law. A human right is damaged here.

Repression under the form of more severe punishment has always been a bad way to bring about solutions. Repression is suppression and suppression leads to even more anger and hate. Throughout history we have seen that large groups of people and individuals seek an outcome for these feelings of frustrations. Anger is energy and this energy must be transformed in something constructive. If this is impossible, then this energy will transform itself in frustration and frustration seeks an outcome in something negative and destructive.

There are as many judges as there are people. Everybody has an idea of what he would do for this or that criminal. In general these solutions are repressive. In several states of the United States the death penalty has been restored. As a deterrent it has no value at all. Criminality has not been reduced, on the contrary. Society is relieved of one criminal, but the whole atmosphere linked to the death penalty is one of hostility. People cannot live in a hostile community. Understanding, helpfulness and love avoid much to keep people in line. But a strong word as 'love' has become such a weak subject. Talking about love is 'not done'. Who talks about love!

When the press plays the role of the prosecutor

The days introducing the trial of John, attract hundreds of 'judges'. Supported by the role of the media as 'prosecutor', everybody has an opinion about the outcome of the trial. The majority is in favor of the restoration of the death penalty. Others prefer a torture session of several hours before hanging John the middle of the market place. Others think that castration is an option for justice. Very few choose treatment for such criminals. When they dare speak out loud what they think, they are attacked by the others. The media plays with these strong emotions and feeds the hunger for sensationalism. They spread the most gruesome details about the murders and don't show any compunction concerning the lies and exaggerations that might be contained in their reports, As if the facts are not awful enough! Some journalists are even able to look right through the skull of John to see what he is thinking. John is the incarnation of the devil himself; John loves to shock people; John is arrogant because he doesn't even look at the parents during his trial; John refuses to answer questions at the tribunal etc . . . The media explains in great detail how John committed his crime and especially what he thought in the mean time. The pictures of the children are published on the front pages of the newspapers with their little angel faces next to the face of the devil himself. As in fever they invent new words to feed the hate of the population. The stirred up masses have now become uncontrollable.

Nobody asks himself how John has become what he is now. Nobody looked for the unhappy childhood of that child despite the wealth and material richness in which he had been educated. Of course this is not an excuse for the crime he committed; there is nothing that can excuse this. But we are obliged to look over the sources and reasons of such violent behavior to be able to avoid it in the future. This becomes very difficult when one is led to prejudge, stirred up by the media and mass frenzy.

The masses do not want an explanation, but wants an example for eventual other child killers. As said before, it has no effect on these kinds of killers. They are formed with anger during their whole lives. You cannot erase that with higher sentences. Before and during their crime they don't think about the consequences. The only thing that matters at that point is to fulfill their fantasies and thereby release the stress built up in a lifetime. It is only after the crime that they realize what they have done and that they risk a severe punishment. The fear for punishment can increase the chance that they will kill the prime witness, in these cases: the victim. They do this to avoid that the victim later recognizes them. It cannot be the intention of that repression? Punishments such as castration have no sense either. Many sexual criminals, as John, are impotent and unable to perform the sex act at the moment of the crime. For instance, John raped his victims with all kinds of objects because he was too stressed to have an erection. Castration leads to even more frustrations with all consequences that go with it. I'll explain that later in this book.

John's judgment is already a fact before the trial even started. Also here the media did their 'job' profoundly hunting for every detail and reporting without verifying if what they are writing is true. They contacts all involved family members and takes care that the defense has no space left. John's lawyers have to slip into the Court room like thieves in the back door, because they are threatened with death. Experts that dare talk about therapy for paedosexuals to avoid relapse, are jeered away instantly during the trial. Those who ask for the death penalty are honored and are allowed to explain their point of view for hours. One is in favor or against. There is no room for neutrality and objectivity. Only a few journalists made an effort to examine John's childhood. They point to the danger of a loveless youth and childhood and try to convince the mass that luxury and money are no guarantee for luck. Children, they say, need love and protection to be able to grow up to become stable and well-balanced adults. These journalists are rarities in this media circus.

Most of the press people are looking for sensation. When they explain the details of a crime extensively they don't take into account that what they deliver here is another scenario for other potential child killers. Some sick spirits drink and feed themselves with all these 'juicy' details in the newspapers. Some even copy the Modus Operandi of other killers or they develop a system based on what they have read. Often that scenario would never have crossed their minds if they hadn't read it in black and white in the newspaper. Also the way a criminal is caught is a source of inspiration for other criminals; they will take care not to make the same mistakes.

The media can play an important role in the prevention of child murder. For instance by pointing out what the serious consequences of child maltreatment can be. Maybe we can then reach parents and other caretakers to kick them into awareness when they are violent towards children. The media can also be less tendenscious and report what the possibilities are for paedosexuals. They can explain what treatment means and how they could feel better by obtaining professional treatment.

John's Trial

It is a marvelously sunny day, although there is no reason to be happy about that. Masses of people block the entrance to the Court. The police try to organize everything with barriers. There is almost no place for the public because all the chairs are taken by the press from all over the world. The safety procedures are tremendous. It looks as if they are preparing for a war. Large numbers of police officers armed to the teeth are patrolling around the building. Everybody is examined and controlled. Without a proper justification document you cannot get in. Once inside everybody has to pass by a metal detector. Of course the thing screams every minute. Hands glide mechanically over bodies and control every little corner to look for weapons. My handbag is turn upside down on a table in a heartbeat.

Finally I enter the trial room. Silently I glide onto the bench, some meters from me sits Anne, John's wife. She is on the point of a nervous breakdown. Next to her I see two muscular body guards. They have to guarantee her safety. I feel for her. She looks so fragile and so marked by this drama. She dares not look up. The hate is so palpable here and it is also directed at her. Scared she glances around her, without seeing anything. These must be the most awful days of her life.

In front of the room are many journalists with their cameras at the ready. John has to be brought in. For this trial they installed a specially built glass cage wherein he will be taking his place in a few minutes. The parents of the murdered children are sitting in front of that cage. Just three metres separate them from the man that destroyed their lives in a second. The mother of one of the victims is staring in front of her, her hands clasped tightly. She doesn't seem to hear or see anything. She is one block of pain. Her husband sits next to her. He is as absent as she is. Next to them are the other parents. Their calm is almost unnatural. Nevertheless I don't have the feeling that they are drugged. My brain is blocked by seeing such dignity. They want to see the monster. These people have been prepared for this trial for two years. It will ask an incredible amount of courage from them, but they want to know and to see. They also want to hear the experts that examined the dead bodies of their children. They feel they owe that to their children who have been taken away from them in the most inhuman manner. During the whole trial they are supported by psychiatrists and by their lawyers. They come finally to hear 'why' this man has killed their children. Journalist buzz like flies around their heads. The smallest move of one of the parents provokes a volley of camera flashes.

Exactly on time the president enters the court room. He asks to bring in the accused. Tension is rising to an incredible extent. A side door opens and three police officers bring in John who is handcuffed. He walks bent over and keeps his eyes fixed on the floor. In the cage his handcuffs are removed. He keeps staring at the floor. Flashes are lighting the court room in an unnatural way. Journalists scrabble over each other to get the most sensational picture. I shrink when I look at the parents who observe this murderer of their children. Their faces show no emotions. No hate, no anger, no disgust. The whole happening has something unreal about it. I shrink when I look at John.

After what seemed an eternity I hear the president of the court say to the journalists that the shooting session is over. From now on no more pictures can be taken in the court room. They pull themselves back and seek their places.

The trial is declared officially open. Firstly the names of the jury are read out, eleven men and women. Then the names of the witnesses are called. We are all brought to a separate room. We are not allowed to talk to each other about the case.

Under the pressure of the public opinion the court can do nothing else but give John the maximum sentence. For this trial the punishment for paedosexual crimes had been increased. The lawyers hardly dared defend John and they keep silent for the majority of the time. They only observe so that there are no procedural mistakes made. For them this trial is a major free publicity. Nobody defends John in any way. An important chance to inform people about their responsibility in educating a child is therefore lost. At no time was the subject 'John as a child' discussed. The history of his sister who was also seriously damaged in her childhood is not used. Not even the violence at home. The professor who followed up John's sister for over twenty years to help her survive, made a full report of the causes of all this. His report was not even read in the court room. The lawyers don't even intervene when witnesses declare that John had a 'carefree' youth in Paris. John's mother cannot come to the trial because of her age. His sister is too damaged and too sick to make such a long journey. She cannot bear the tremendous pressure of the trial and the media hassle. His other brothers and sisters dare not come and his adoptive parents (aunt and uncle) refused to come. The president of the court didn't even insist.

Personally I believe that everyone connected with the upbringing of a child murderer should be with him on trial when proven that they are responsible for maltreating, abandoning, hitting, exploiting and abusing their child in the past.

John is sentenced to thirty years in prison followed by thirty years of probation in the State of France. He will never be free again. Locking up people like John and then quietly closing our eyes is not the solution to avoid these kinds of crimes.

"Send me the tape of Michael Jackson" John once wrote to me after the trial. I asked him why. He likes the song 'Heal the world' and he likes Michael Jackson. "We are the same. They accuse him of child sex abuse, but they forget that Michael does so much for children."

"What do you mean by this, John. Is it an excuse for abusing children."

"You people always look at the bad side, but there is also a good side. He helps many children too."

"Thousands of children saved by Michael Jackson do not excuse one abuse, John. I'm sorry. I heard this excuse so many times: 'the poor man helped so many elderly' and then one day he is convicted for raping five little girls, 'the poor man played Santa Claus for the whole city' while they found thirty bodies of young men and boys buried in his basement. You use this 'helping' to not attract attention to your perverted activities. You also try to cover your crimes and it is a very manipulative way to turn away suspicions. Who would think that this good man would harm somebody? So anyway you don't do it for the others, you do it for yourselves, and by the way, why Michael Jackson?"

"Because we can recognize each other."

"How?"

"For instance, in the way we look at children. I can see it in the way other paedosexuals observe and look at children. They all have the same look. A bit glazed."

"Fantasizing?"

"You could call it that, anyway I saw at least ten other paedosexuals in that courtroom."

"Interesting."

The Bachmeyer case

Fifteen years ago the seven year old daughter of Marianne Bachmeyer has been raped and strangled. The murderer has been arrested a few days later.

Very soon it was clear that this criminal was a re-offender. After an earlier prison sentence for raping another little girl, the court decided he had to be 'made impotent' by a doctor. After his prison sentence he was free. He didn't have any form of psychological treatment or follow up and he has been released in reality, into a world that rejected him, with a mind full of overloaded perverted fantasies.

He went to see a doctor and invented a story about being impotent. The doctor who knew anything about his past, gave him a prescription to increase his potency. Four days later he raped the seven year old girl. Out of fear for punishment he strangled her and hid her little body in an old dresser in a garden. The girl had been found there some days later.

Not only was information about the killer reported in the media, but also information about the mother of the victim. All kind of gossips about her private life, even down to the smallest detail was spread over the newspapers. These self declared judges reproached her that she was not a good mother: she stayed out late at night and her little girl had to make breakfast for herself before going to school.

During the trial Marianne Bachmeyer bought herself a gun and put it on the kitchen table. She wanted to make clear to the killer that she would be waiting for him at the prison gate when he is released in thirty years. All these years he would have to live in fear for what would happen when he has finished his sentence.

The first three days of the trial Marianne was in serious doubt of what to do: take the gun with her or leave it on the kitchen table? Her anger grew. The killer was not only responsible for the murder of her child, but also for the bad stories in the media that besmirched her good name and her reputation.

The fourth day of the trial she took the gun with her into the court room. The first three days the murderer didn't open his mouth. The fourth day he did speak. As in trance Marianne, outwardly calm but inwardly a much stressed woman, heard how the criminal started to blame her little girl. Her child would have asked for sex with a totally strange man! Her child challenged him! Her child seduced him! It was not his fault. She couldn't listen to this anymore. Like a robot she stood up and walked slowly through the overcrowded court room to the front. She took her place right in front of the killer and looked him straight in the eyes while she clasped the gun in her right hand in her pocket. Without hesitating she then took her hand out of her pocket, pointed the gun at the forehead of the killer and fired. She continued to fire until the gun was empty. Panic broke loose. Blood spurted in all directions. The killer murmured something and then collapsed behind the stand. Nobody had time to react. For Marianne justice had been done.

I met her years later during a television show in the Netherlands. It was a program on child killings. I asked her why she had done what she did. She smiled calmly and started to talk:

"I can and will not judge what others should do. For me it was at that time the only thing I could do. Maybe it is not the same for others. There is room for everything: for grief, for anger, for pain and for healing. At the moment I killed the murderer of my child, I already had months of grief and incredible pain. The first three days of the trial the grief was still there and at the same time there was more space for anger. Anger about this man and anger for what the media had spread about me and my little girl. Finally the ultimate point of anger came when he suddenly started to sneer and degrade my baby, this, after he hadn't opened his mouth for three days. I couldn't let this happen."

Her case shocked Germany and she served several years of prison. Did she have any regrets?

"No. I never regretted what I did. I wouldn't advise others to do it, but I know that this solution was for me the only right one at that moment. I understand people who can forgive. I understand people who try to live with their grief. But for me it was different. Everybody lives his drama in his own way. I cannot give advice on this."

When I asked her if the press reports had had any influence on what she decided to do, she said it was not the case: not in the way that it prompted her to revenge her daughter, but it did incite her inner anger. She couldn't stand to listen to so many lies about her and her girl in the media. She had no voice in all of this. Her neighbors and friends had been interviewed many times. The killer had his say in this, but nobody ever asked her anything, and they continued writing those lies. Seen from this point of view, the press did their 'job' well.

Again we can see the consequences of an inadequate approach to sexual criminals, the sensational slant of the media and the lack of support for parents of victims. How parents deal with all this, doesn't seem to be the concern or responsibility of anyone.

CHAPTER 3

An International Approach

There is an absolute need of according law systems in Europe to avoid this tremendous problem. There is not one country where the same law is used to sanction paedosexuals. The policy concerning child murder is different in every country. This gives paedosexuals great opportunities. They have no problems with country borders, they can only have a problem with the language in the different countries. Most of the criminals have to approach their victims first and so they must be able to speak the language of the victims. Multilinguistic criminals find victims in different countries. So they take advantage of the judicial situation in each country. When we take a closer look at Marc Dutroux who killed at least four victims in eighteen months in Belgium, we see that two of the victims he chose came from the Dutch speaking part of the country. Julie and Melissa, two eight year old little girls had been abducted not far from where he lived. Then he took An and Eefje two hundred kilometers from where he lived in the Dutch speaking part of the country. When those four victims were dead, he abducted another child at approximately hundreds kilometers from home, again in the French speaking part of the country and five months later he took Laetitia also some distance from home. The two last girls survived months of imprisonment in his basement. The case shocked the entire world especially because of the incompetence of the police departments and the lack of communication between the different services. The French speaking police could not communicate with the Dutch speaking police. They didn't even make an effort to contact them. The Dutch speaking police who do make the effort to speak the other language, did contact the French speaking but communication went awfully wrong. And then there are also the different jurisdictional departments. The killer knew this. He took advantage of this situation to stay out of the hand of the authorities. Especially because he had an extensive criminal record for the similar crimes he had committed before.

Recently another serial killer has been arrested in Belgium for the abduction of a little girl. She was able to escape by jumping out of the driving car. It took months before the police realized that they were looking at a serial killer. His wife came to the station and told them her husband had killed several girls. His name is Michel Fourniret and he is French. When it became too hot for him in France, he moved to Belgium. Nobody checked his criminal record and so he could go on killing and raping. He killed at least ten women. He has admitted to nine murders up to now. One girl stays unknown. Fourniret's wife told the police that her husband had also killed a babysitter somewhere in 1992. The girl has never been identified. Maybe she was English? Did Belgium contact England to find this out? They did check for France and until now no young woman fitted the profile of the murdered girl. Fourniret refuses to tell where he hid the body.

In England there is a child killer in prison for the murder of eleven children. He also killed three children in France, two in the Netherlands and one in Germany. The other countries are unable to make these links because of the bad or nonexistent cooperation between the different countries. This must be heaven for criminals and many of them know that.

I contacted a police officer in the Netherlands. He had a connection with the F.B.I. in the U.S.A. I informed him of the facts I had gathered and described the precise Modus Operandi of this particular child killer. I asked him if he would look for cold cases in the South of the Netherlands. Some weeks later he called me back and said that indeed he found two cases that could be linked to the killer in England. It took a long time to proceed with these cases because the English authorities were not so keen on receiving a commission of another country. This could damage the reputation of a country, and then there are the exhausting procedures to keep everything legally correct. It is imperative that the whole system is reviewed to make it easier to cooperate in this United Europe of today.

While justice departments fight to get every letter of the law right, parents live for years in uncertainty and fear about the fate of their children.

It is my opinion that it is not normal that a crime can profit from the well known term of limitation. Parents have no message to this. I know parents who are looking for their children for tens of years. For them it will never end, no matter what the law is doing.

The case of Johnny White

Johnny White is a little baby when he is put into an orphanage after his parents died in a car accident. His youth seems to have been spent in a normal manner there. He learns the profession of butcher but that is only a façade. Behind this grows, just as we have seen with John, a cluster of anger. It is difficult to find out what really happened in his childhood after so many years. Johnny collects porn and fills in every free moment watching porn films.

His crime career starts at the age of sixteen. The first time he succeeds in abducting a little girl he is amazed that the child follows him with eyes full of trust. She follows him like a little puppy to a remote area. There he grabs the child and starts to touch her. The little girl is shocked and starts to scream. Neighbors come running and grab the little girl out of his hands.

The judge limits his intervention to a small correction because the adolescent continues to deny the facts. No follow up, no treatment, no communication.

Two years later again he abducts a child of six. For this crime he is given a prison sentence by the court.

At the age of twenty two he leaves prison without having once been seen by a psychiatrist. He is more disturbed and dangerous then ever before, but nobody notices.

Johnny has no address and so he moves in with friends in the North of London. His friends rent him a very little room. One day one of the children of that family finds masses of porn under Johnny's bed. The little boy tells his parents and Johnny has to leave the house instantly. On a regular basis Johnny went to the Netherlands to buy child porn.

From that moment on it is difficult to reconstruct Johnny's movements. He rents furnished rooms all over the country.

Finally, in 1982, he finds a job as a decorator of publicity panels along the roads. This job makes it easy to travel around the whole country. Because Johnny lives alone and is incapable of taking care of himself, his colleagues start to name him 'Johnny the stinker'. Johnny doesn't know how to defend himself, just as John didn't and so many other child killers that I examined in all these years. He closes himself up in his fantasy world where he is the winner. He accepts every possible job and he doesn't mind working every weekend. Anyway, he has no family waiting for him and he has never had friends to go out with.

At the 30th of July 1982 eleven year old Susan disappears. She was on her way to play tennis that afternoon, but she never arrived. Fourteen days later her body is found 350 km from the place of her disappearance. The girl was raped, strangled and her face was destroyed with vitriol, a biting acid. Then the criminal had set fire to her body.

In July 1983 five year old Caroline disappears. In March 1986, Sarah who went to buy bread didn't come home. Both girls were find: raped, strangled and their faces destroyed with vitriol. Both were burned.

Only one victim managed to escape in a miraculous way. Fifteen year old Theresa fought like a lion to save her life when Johnny tried to drag her into his car in 1988. He had to let her go.

In 1990 he grabbed a little five year old girl. Over all these years he adapted his Modus Operandi: at first he drives his van slowly alongside his chosen victim. He counts the rhythm of her steps and then drives ten meters further. He then parks the car and waits while he continues to count her steps in his head. Without leaving his van he crawls to the back of it and waits inside by the sliding door. All the time he carries on counting and so he knows when the victim reaches the level of the door. He pulls the door open, grabs the child and closes the door again. It is a matter of seconds. In his van, full of publicity boards, lies also a sleeping bag. He pushes the victim in head first and closes the sleeping bag. The child cannot escape. Then he looks for a quiet place where he can continue his macabre game.

That same year he is caught in the act by a woman who was cleaning her windows. He drove by and took a little five year old girl. The woman cannot believe her eyes. The van suddenly disappears and the girl she just saw walking along the street also. She feels something is wrong but everything happened so fast that she had doubts about what she had seen. She decides to run to a police car at the corner of the street and to warn them. The police react instantly and with wailing sirens they follow the indicated van. They succeed in ramming the car and they get the child unconscious but alive out of the sleeping bag.

Ray Wire of the Gracewell Institute of Birmingham (here over more in the next chapter) has long conversations with the criminal in prison. He told me that Johnny also found victims on the continent. I do some research and indeed I find several unsolved cases in France. Three little girls had been murdered and the crimes carry the signature of Johnny. When he drove to the Netherlands to buy child porn he used his professional van. He took the boat to Calais in France. Then he drove over Belgium to the Netherlands. It is possible that Johnny also abducted children in Belgium.

On a Sunday in May 1987 the ten year old Virginia played with her friend in the front garden before going to her Sunday class. She lives with her family in a quiet little village near Paris. Virginia disappears from the garden. Three weeks later eleven year old Sophie disappears at approximately twenty kilometers from where Virginia disappeared. It only took a few minutes. Sophie was on her way to the chemist to get some paint to finish the painting she was doing. She only had hundreds meters to walk. She disappeared without a trace. Her parents quickly alerted the police and immediately a search is started. That same evening her body is found on a remote parking area. Only a few days after the murder of Sophie, the seven year old Perrinne is lost. This abduction takes place at forty kilometers from where Sophie and Virginia disappeared. Perrine's body is found three weeks later in a field. The day Perrine's body is found nine year old Sabrina disappears six kilometers from that last crime scene. She is on her way to the bookstore to get her favorite magazine. It is only a ten meter walk. A witness declares that he saw Sabrina at the funfair nearby. So she didn't walk home immediately. The witness saw her with a big, heavy man. Two days later her body is found in a ravine. Just as the other children, Sabrina is raped, strangled and her face is burned away with acid. Finally the body of the first French victim is found in a field the 9th of October 1987.

Hundreds of inhabitants of the area are questioned by the police but nothing can help the investigation any further. The police decide that it cannot be someone from the area. It doesn't cross anyone's mind that it might be someone who is not French. The witnesses are formal: every time a child disappeared, a white van has been noticed in the area. Johnny sometimes spends his holidays with acquaintances in France.

Johnny White is convicted in England for life. When we list his crimes it looks as follows:

First victim in England:	1963
Second victim in England:	1965
Third victim in England:	1967
Fourth victim in England:	July 1982
Fifth victim in England:	July 1983
Sixth victim in England:	March 1986
Seventh victim in England:	9 May 1987
Eighth victim in France:	30 May 1987
Ninth victim in France:	3 June 1987
Tenth victim in France:	27 June 1987
Eleventh victim in England:	12 April 1990

We can observe that the urge to commit a crime the first years appear with an interval of two years. Suddenly we see a pause of fifteen years. Then two crimes and again several years of non activity. Then the frequency increases till June 1987. Again a lull of three years. For a child killer this is an abnormal pattern. Everything makes us believe that he also killed children in this period of time but that the link to him hasn't been made. Unfortunately I don't have the dates of the crimes in the Netherlands and Germany. But because nothing appears between 1987 and 1990 it is obvious that files of unsolved child murders and disappearances have to be dug up all over Europe. Johnny was not in prison those years, nor was he sick or temporary excluded for whatever reason.

When we take in account the frequency of killings in 1987, it is impossible that he was able to control himself during those three silent years. In his 'acute' phases he committed four child murders in the space of six weeks!

I examined a child killer in France from whom I can practically say with certainty that he killed children over the whole continent and probably even over the whole world. When he lived in the USA he was often under an enormous pressure. The scenario of stress and the hereby fitting consequences have been explained extensively in this book. I contacted the FBI in Quantico and asked them to look for missing children in the period of time between 1987 and 1988. I made a report about the killer and his Modus Operandi. My correspondent at the FBI put every element in his computer and the case is under investigation. They had no idea of the killer in Europe and his stay in their country.

The FBI has for many years worked with the VICAP-system. VICAP stands for Violent Criminal Apprehension Program. Thanks to this program they can better understand the sources of violent crimes. It also helps to analyze crimes and make a profile of the killer. A mass of information is gathered and is based on twenty years of research to get an insight into the world of this kind of criminal. How was his childhood, how was his family, what are his thinking patterns, how did he prepare his crime and more importantly, how can we catch him?

This system has been developed with the cooperation of different police services from fieldworker to the highest level of investigators. At the basis of this incredibly well documented system lays people such as Robert K. Ressler, Ann W. Burgess and John E. Douglas.

Robert Ressler is the man who made the term 'serial killer' known all over the world. He studied criminology and was one of the directors of the

Forensic Behavioral Services who trained, consulted and formed witness experts. He is an FBI veteran who worked for more than twenty years for his police department. For sixteen years he was part of the Behavioral Science Unit, where worked at the improvement and the renovation of many programs which finally resulted in the NCAVC-program. NCAVC stands for National Centre for the Analysis of Violent Crime. He is also the founder of the VICAP system.

Ann Burgess founded the crisis-intervention-hospital for rape victims. She is an authority in the field of inter-family violence. She was also the chief investigator in the investigation of child pornography, sexual murders and patterns in crimes. She is often indicated by the authorities to help as an expert in very serious crimes. She also is a co-author of the book: Sexual Homicide, Patterns and Motives.

John Douglas is head inspector at the FBI and had his professional experience in Detroit and Milwaukee. He too was a co-worker at the NCAVC department. He specialized in investigations of arson crimes where the criminals use explosives. In the USA, Canada, Puerto Rico, England, Australia, Central-America and Italy he worked on more than 5.000 crimes.

These people have a multitude of information that they want to share with other countries. Working with them is a real pleasure. The teams are composed with motivated investigators who are ready to specialize in diverse branches of criminality. Their willingness to cooperate should be an example for their colleagues in Europe.

Very specific questionnaires are compiled by people working in crime and murder cases. (See extension 1) Each informant is important and is taken very seriously. The information and observations in each crime is transferred to the NCAVC. There this information is analyzed and sorted by crime. The character qualities and the outer marks of criminals are stored in computer programs. They all use this information to help solve unsolved crimes. In the meantime they continue reassembling every piece of information possible. This helps to keep track of the evolution of society and the eventual changes in the diverse techniques of criminals. It is important to keep a record of what is going on in crime environments.

Unfortunately we see that the authorities on the continent aren't very keen to change their system. Everybody that shows the will and the perseverance to work in an effective way are systematically excluded. The government is lazy and slow and doesn't want to see the urgency of the situation. Since the Dutroux scandal things have changed for the good, but it is sad to see that we needed this to make those changes, and there's still so much to do. One thing is sure: the authorities have been awakened with a tremendous shock. Not so much about the tragedy but especially about the damages done to the country because the whole world was in shock when it saw the incompetence and the arrogance of the police departments. Especially the inhumanity in which parents and family members had been approached by the authorities for so many years. Almost 500.000 people marched in the streets of Brussels. Not so much because of the horror of Dutroux himself and what he had done to the victims, but especially because the population was disgusted with the way it is treated by the authorities. In an attempt to calm down the feelings of the population that almost destroyed the court houses in every city, they formed the missing child unit 'Child Focus', and units to guarantee the follow up of paedosexuals were installed all over the country. Unfortunately nobody was professionally trained to work with offenders or even know what a child sex offender is, but it is a start and time will learn and teach. We can only hope that the attention will not fade away with time, because child sex abuse is the most awful damage that can be done to a child. Later we will discuss the figures about the past of child sex offenders and child killers.

PART V

Therapy and Prevention

CHAPTER I

The Gracewell Institute of Birmingham

The Gracewell Institute of Birmingham is a centre for the treatment of paedosexuals. It is a beautiful building promising rest and warmth. I have seen several therapists with different backgrounds. This is one of the most famous centers in the world. Only 3 % of the child sex offenders relapse. Without treatment most of them relapse within a period of four days on average.

Ray Wire first worked as a prison guard. He was amazed that he always saw the same criminals coming back for the same offences, especially child sex offenders. To get a better insight into their problems he started to talk with those men. He understood that most of them are unable to cope with life in society. In prison they are more at ease. Living in a closed society is easy. Everything is done for them. Life is so much easier than outside. They don't have to make decisions in prison, others do that for them. For the child, they have always been, it is the easy way. Complicated situations upset them, they get tense and their behavior becomes impossible and their environment rejects them. We have already seen what this feeling of rejection provokes.

A few years ago Ray Wire decided to study this specific deviant behavior. He had some specialized courses and surrounded himself with skilled therapists. Soon he opened the Gracewell Institute. It is a closed centre. Paedosexuals live there and are only allowed to leave the centre with permission from their therapist and then accompanied by a staff member. A maximum of twenty five criminals can be in treatment. They are considered as 'clients' and not as 'patients' because paedosexuals are not sick people. When described as patients we give them an excuse for their deviant behavior: "We are sick, so it is not our responsibility."

The Institute teaches them that they are indeed responsible for their actions and they can learn how to control their behavior. With the therapists the client searches for solutions for his deviancy, he learns how to control his impulses. Role plays are very helpful in this. Therein they learn how they have to deal with a problem in an adult way instead of storing all their feelings inside and finally explode in abusive behavior.

Firstly they have to pass the assessment phases. It takes an average of four weeks. In this period of time the staff evaluates if the client opens up for treatment. Depending on the seriousness of the deviancy they decide who is accepted for the intensive treatment program. Some paedosexuals cannot be helped. People who do not use excuses to justify their behavior are very difficult to treat. They have no notion of the difference between good and bad. They don't find child sex abuse good or bad either. It is something they do, so what is the problem? Those who are not allowed for treatment are sent back to prison.

After the four week assessment session the real treatment starts for an average of two years. It is a period of intensive hard work. The entire personality structure of the paedosexual is professionally unraveled because it is built around lies and fantasies and has nothing to do with reality. Unravel and rebuild. These men have convinced themselves for so many years that what they do is completely justified. Therefore they use all kinds of excuses. "I'm never lucky." Or "Everybody is against me." are excuses professionals hear all the time. It makes abusing children easier for them, more acceptable.

We call it reaction-challenging behavior. The offender feels bad and being bad makes it so much easier to take revenge on a child.

Practice placement

In the summer of 1993 I had some weeks of practice placement. I met a woman there, a farmer, who works as a therapist on a part-time contract. Before she worked there she had no practice in this field, but her gift of listening, the fact that she doesn't judge and stays neutral in the approach of the clients, makes her a dream therapist. She is so good at her job and works with perseverance to gain the trust of the clients, under the supervision of more skilled therapists she does a marvelous job.

During my stay there I met two English colleagues with whom I immediately had a terrific contact. Colin is responsible for a centre for sexually abused children in Bradford. To gain a better insight in what they feel and to be able to better help them, he wants to know about the thinking patterns and behavior of paedosexuals. Yvonne is responsible for a Mental Health Centre in Kent. She is confronted with the fact that more and more paedosexuals are sent to her clinic. The government wants to classify them as 'mentally ill' because they don't know what to do with them, because Yvonne doesn't know what to do with them either, she decided to better her understanding of this problem.

At nine in the morning a bus arrives with the paedosexuals who live a few kilometers away. The morning therapy takes five hours. Immediately Yvonne and I are sent in to work with a group of clients. Yvonne takes her place at the board in the front of the room. The first client is David. David abused his daughter for many years. Elly ran away from home to Australia when she was twenty. She was unable to build a decent relationship with a man and felt that the source of that problem lay in the sexual abuse of many years with her father. She was unable to get over this trauma alone and she sought professional help. Her therapist advised her to make a complaint against her father.

It all began when Elly was eight years old. She remembers it as if it was yesterday. Her father took her to his workroom where he forced her to look at pornographic material. She didn't like this and felt embarrassed. But her father forced her again and again and wanted her to feel comfortable about looking at those pictures he spread on a table. He always repeated that she was his little princess and that he had chosen her. They had their little secret and nobody was allowed to know about it. Elly didn't like that secret. She really felt bad about it. She felt dirty, used and especially confused and not at all like a princess from the fairy tales she used to read about, Princesses were happy, she wasn't. She was not allowed to have girl friends, she was not allowed to go with mummy to the shop or the market. Daddy was always around. She had to touch him, caress him and play all kinds of dirty games with him. And above all: she had to keep her mouth shut. A leaden secret weighed on her shoulders, it became her companion. Fear became her closest friend.

Nights changed into dangerous monsters, because he would come in the dark. If he would come or leave her alone, she never knew. So she stayed vigilant. Terrified she listened to every sound in the house, she was frightened by any noise on the stairs and was relieved when the morning came. In the morning she was exhausted but had to go to school. At least there she was safe from his grabbing fingers. The web closed more and more around her. There was no escape route. Nobody noticed and nobody asked questions. Daddy reassured Elly time after time that what they did was normal. All daddies do this with their children. For years this hell went on. She became a young woman and the fear of getting pregnant plagued her. Her father bought her a solarium, hush-money. It was worse than this, but Elly would only discover this much later, by coincidence. It was late that evening and already dark when she came into her room. She couldn't find the switch immediately but she could see small rays of light that seemed to come from different points in the wall. She started to look around in the dark and discovered to her dismay little holes in the wall. Behind this wall was the workroom of her father. Father was there because there was light. He drilled those holes to peep at his daughter when she was nude under the solarium. There was simply no place in this damned house where she was safe. Always and everywhere he was spying on her. He created opportunities to isolate her from the rest of the family.

Physically this girl may have survived, but mentally and emotionally she is severely damaged and it could take years to restore herself assurance and self esteem to make her able to trust adults again. For the moment she works to heal and part of this healing process means that her father has to be punished and re-educated for what he has done.

David is now in front of Yvonne by the board. He has to tell the group what he has done. He does this because he has to, not because he thinks he has a problem that he has to work on. This we can hear in the way he tells his story. When he finishes his story, he is relieved. He thinks that the worse part is over. It is not. Yvonne asks him in a friendly way to write the story down on the board. This is the second confrontation with what he has done. The first was verbal, this one is visual. He has to write his crimes down in black and white. It is difficult for him. He tries to gain time. Yvonne encourages him, stays next to him and corrects him when he tries to cover reality. The naked truth and nothing more has to be put on the board. When David finally finished, he sighs again. He hopes that it is the end and he already makes an attempt to go and sit in the group. Yvonne asks him nicely to stay and to read what he has just written down. This is the third confrontation with his crimes in an hour. This confrontation is auditory. He hears himself say what he has done to his daughter. Yvonne underlines several crucial words and turns then to the group to ask which words they find interesting to examine. David shrinks by the minute. He stares at the floor. He is thinking of excuses to justify his behavior or at least to minimize his responsibility. Every underlined word is discussed, David has to explain the why's and the who's and the what's. When Yvonne doubts the truth of his explanation she turns to the group and asks if David's explanation is relevant. Because these paedosexuals are stuck in an infantile stage of their emotional development, they react as children and are as merciless as children can be. So it isn't a surprise that they can be very hard on each other. Every lie is uncovered. David is confronted with his lies until he admits that he tries to show things differently.

While Yvonne leads the session, I observe the group of eight offenders. I register their body language and I also observe the absurd explanations in the story. I also observe those who do not participate enough in the discussion and those who try to draw too much attention to them. I also note the points that have not been discussed and that can be used in the next session. This first session takes about two hours, after which we have a short break. The group can go and have a cup of coffee or tea while we have a meeting in the office where we can examine the video tapes of the session. During the next hour we discuss further strategy, taking into account all the remarks made the first time. When the group comes back we work intensively on the destruction of the big lie that controls their whole lives.

At noon we have lunch, even then it is interesting to observe the group of offenders. It is immediately clear how much difficulty they have to make contact with each other. Most of them are sitting reading or smoking a cigarette. Very few talk to each other. They all seem a bit introverted.

After lunch, we start again with the whole group. It is my turn to lead the session. I introduce myself and I tell them I am from Belgian. I make it clear right away that if I make a mistake or I don't explain properly, I want them to tell me immediately. English is not my language and I want to avoid the fact that they might use this to say that they didn't understand what I meant. The experience show that they will take every opportunity they can grab to not have to answer 'difficult' questions.

I ask David to return to the accusations again.
"They say I abused my daughter for fourteen years."
"They?"
"My daughter pretends this is so. She made a complaint against me and moved to Australia. If I don't agree to have treatment in this centre here, I have to go to prison."
"And? Did you abuse her?"
"... yes ..."
"Tell me how it started."
"Well, it started when she was eight years old. I told her that she was my favorite daughter. That she was so special to me. After a while I trapped her in my workroom. There I hid my pornographic books and I wanted her to get used to real life."
"What was in those books, David?"
"... Pictures of men with erections ..." David looks down at the floor.

"Do you think this is appropriate material for an eight year old girl?"
"She didn't seem to care. She liked looking at it." He hastens to add.
"How did you notice that?"
". . ."
He stares at the floor, unable to answer that question.

I turn to the group: "Do you all think that this is literature suitable for a little girl?"

"He lies. David does this in first instance to see how far he can go with the child. If she runs away, he knows that his tactic is wrong. He arouses just himself with it. When he sees that the child isn't responding, he won't go further." says Cliff from the group. The others nod their heads in agreement. Very soon the whole group agrees that David knew exactly what he was doing and that this was not appropriate material for a little girl. This step belongs to the 'grooming' phase.

"David, was there something you noticed by your daughter's reaction that she didn't want to see this?"

". . . mmmm . . . yes, she pushed the magazines away and wanted to go to play. She looked bored and ashamed."

The following hour everything is analyzed. At the end of the session David has to copy everything written on the board into his own workbook. So he will see and follow his evolution over time.

A therapy week is planned on a vast scale and needs the utmost concentration. Every word is important; the way it is said, the context in which it stays, the accents used and especially the meaning of what is said. Nothing can escape to the attention of the professional. But the experience is very fascinating. Things are called by their names. The offenders learn to ask questions about their own behavior and attitude. This might seem normal, but believe me it is a really difficult task for those who are not used to doing so. People can be so fixed in a thinking pattern and it can be very frightening to change and let go that pattern. They have convinced themselves for many years that what they do is alright and when they are challenged to see the other side of the coin for a change, the result can be surprising. Most of the men break at that point and are then ready to make fundamental changes in themselves. The results of such a working method are stunning.

Yvonne is a soft, patient woman, but she isn't a person to be trifled with. With growing admiration I observe her when she takes her client with her in her logic. He doesn't seem to be aware of it, but he walks in one straight line after her. As soon as he dares to put a foot to the right or the left, Yvonne is there to grab him gently by his neck and bring him back into line again. Escape is impossible. Just like a cat that doesn't want to hurt its kittens, but will impose her will, Yvonne goes further. Her memory works faultlessly. When necessary she confronts David with his own declarations and cites what he said an hour earlier.

The atmosphere is quiet, not judgmental and not hostile at all. These are frightened children in adult bodies

The therapists work in a role with each other and with two. My second colleague, Colin, has a different working method than Yvonne. I admire his technique, but it isn't my style. He dares to denigrate, shout, force and be authoritarian. His client for the day is Robert. Robert is slavish and he almost literally repeats what has been said to him. He does this to flatter everybody. He doesn't see for himself what is wrong with sexually abusing a child. Different therapists have approached Robert in different ways: nothing helps. Colin tries the tough approach using denigration and anger. He profiles himself as almighty to get a grip on Robert. He wants Robert to feel how it is to be a victim. How the victim felt with him. He forces Robert on the ground and makes him look up to him. He is demanding from high up there.

"Well, Robert? How do you feel down there?" he sneers. Robert fixes his gaze on the floor. "Bad" he says. He says that because he knows that everybody is expecting this from him. In fact it really doesn't affect him at all, it is like water off a duck's back. He is a 'hard' one. Four weeks of observation and evaluation have had no result whatsoever. This is troubling. He will relapse, that's for sure. But Colin doesn't give up. He drops to the floor and imitates Robert. He twitches his face in a pitiful grimace and mourns: "Bad. It feels bad . . . Is that so Robert! Does it feel bad? How bad does it feel then? How bad did Elaine feel when she had to look up at your naked body? How bad must Susan have felt when you forced her to take your penis into her mouth? And Sarah? She was only three years old! How did you feel? You up there, high above them?! How bad does it feel, Robert!"

"Yes, it must have been hard for those kids," squeaks Robert.

"Bad?! Bad?! It was terrifying!" roars Colin. "Again and again it was hell for these children, Robert! YOU were the monster for them! The monster that forced his most perverted fantasies on their defenseless bodies!"

The whole scene is almost pathetic. Robert still stares blankly at the floor. He lies hardly two meters from my feet. I feel sickened by this performance. I feel a powerless anger bubbling up when I look at this pathetic man on the floor. Anger, but anger tinged with compassion. And compassion is the worst feeling I can have in such a situation. I then fall into the trap that Robert is waiting for.

The tension is cutting. Colin continues to crawl around Robert, alternating between intimidation, humiliation and denigration. Sometimes Robert looks angrily at Colin and that is about the only facial expression I can detect in this man.

I carefully observe the other offenders in the group. I see no reaction or emotion, nor compassion for the man at our feet. They don't empathize with this man on the floor. The silence is heavy. Robert's face is transfigured with pain. He grabs his back with both hands. I see that he is really suffering, but I'm also aware that the inner pain is much sharper than the pain in his back. The inside directed pain I am not allowed to see. Nobody is. He is ashamed of that pain. He too has been sexually abused as a child, but men are not supposed to show emotional suffering. That is the way he was educated and that is the way he will be for the rest of his life. Colin used this short intermezzo to prepare another attack.

"Pain." Colin shakes his head: "Do you really know what pain is? Sarah, that child knows what pain means. It is inside and it can not come out. Susan has been crying with pain for so many years. Did you see that pain while you abused them?" Robert shakes his head: No.

"Why should we listen to your pain?" snaps Colin. Robert doesn't answer anymore, he has dissociated. The session is closed.

We do not only have group sessions in the Gracewell Institute. We also have daily consultations with clients. During these individual sessions they find the opportunity to talk about their inner pain and anxiety. They have to do homework for therapy and they have to read books that will be discussed. Every day the clients have to fill in their diary and the following day the contents are discussed with the therapist.

In the residence they learn how to behave as an adult in conflicting situations. Each of them is given a task like washing the dishes, making the beds, cooking dinner, cleaning etc. They each have their own room where they can be alone and do their therapeutic homework.

Every month an actor comes to direct the role play. He has had specialized training to work with sex offenders and so he knows what to do with these clients. For the paedosexual this is the most painful part of his program. Here he will learn empathy. He has to put himself completely into the victim's shoes to understand the impact of his acts. They are very emotional scenes. And finally discussions are organized with the probation officers to discuss the evolution of each client. Each client has to make a list of at least forty people who are aware of his crimes, These people are also involved in the therapy to show how they can keep a social control on the offender when he is set free. It seems a terrifying and draconic measure, but it isn't. All these people are trained to understand the specific problem of child sex abuse. They learn how to recognize the first alarm signals, so the client can be warned about his first step to relapse before it is too late. Besides, the client can always fall back on the centre for help or support. In some cases he can come back to restart a part of the therapy and the techniques he learned to control himself.

Unfortunately the Gracewell Clinic has been destroyed by firebombs when the local community found out that the clinic was a treatment centre for child sex offenders. For many years it wasn't known to the public but after a television programme on child sex offenders, the clinic was shown as a model. Then everybody knew what happened there and someone decided to destroy the whole project. This is understandable but incredibly sad because it also shows that the public doesn't know what a child sex offender is and how important it is to treat them instead of just locking them away in prison without proper treatment.

CHAPTER 2

An Efficient Approach

Therapy and guidance.

Child sex offenders are taught what risk situations are. They have to learn how to avoid these situations. If unfortunately they are confronted with such problems, they have to know what they have to do. A risk situation is for instance that he is alone at home with a very young child, or if he also feels depressive at that moment, or a bit down, the step to relapse to a new crime is easily made. Because he was able to find excuses for so many years it will be easy for him to convince himself that for ones it isn't so bad and that the child asks for it by staying alone in the house. Luckily he learned in his therapy sessions to use his brakes to correct his behavior in the early stages.

The professional secret cannot be used for child sex offenders. It is just this secret that makes it so difficult to get this tremendous problem out of the shadow. It is thanks to all the secrets around the offences that these sorts of criminals succeed in staying out of the hands of the Justice Departments.

A contract of non-confidentiality with his therapist is thus a must. It is also a security key that the therapist cannot hide behind professional secrecy to not take responsibility in this. It is thus absolutely necessary that the therapist discusses the relapses and the progress of the client with his environment and his probation officer. I personally discuss my clients' files with his lawyer and eventually with the prosecutor in his case. When the client is in probation and released or he is free while he is awaiting his trial he is obliged to come in for therapy, I will always make it very clear that when he doesn't come for his sessions his lawyer will be contacted. His lawyer has to announce this unwillingness to the prosecutor. A decision to take the client into custody should be taken quickly to keep our society safe. After his prison sentence he can then come back into therapy. It is a bit like a stick behind the door, but to protect children one should do everything possible. Paedosexuals do not stop on their own initiative. No matter what they say, it is not true! The relapse figures float around 90 % and one can easily say that the other 10 % is just not caught.

An Impasse

What happens when the therapy ends up in an impasse? An impasse with an especially aggressive client is the result of incomplete knowledge of their clinical problem. At the basis of this impasse lays the incompetence of the therapist. He or she has not been sufficiently alert and was unable to calculate if the client was trying to lock him or her up in a specific thinking pattern. J. Chasseguet-Smirnel, psychiatrist, often talks about the importance of a complete psychical examination of the client. He underlines how a client can manipulate and attack the thinking patterns of a therapist. This has the consequence of the therapist becoming unable to think straight. When the client succeeds in this partially or completely, the therapy is in an impasse. The client will not feel safe on an emotional level and will become aggressive on a verbal and physical level. Because physical violence is the only way he learned to elucidate a problem. It is his only way out. The therapist sees himself/herself in a situation wherein he or she has to let go, paralyzed with fear. There are little possibilities left to evaluate the sources and the breeding ground of these aggressive attacks. Possibly he or she changes his/her therapeutic approach and will continue the treatment in an atmosphere of complete denial. Paralyzed by this impasse the therapist can not discuss the fear and frustration with the client anymore. His increasing worry about this evolution will lead to the fact that he is unable to perceive the elements that are linked to the aggressive attacks of the client. It becomes difficult to draw limits. The therapists as well as the clients become prisoners in their roles. The therapist is captured in this impasse. The only thing he can do is to stick to a systematic approach to get out of this situation.

The evaluation of a violent client always exposes the therapist to contratranferential traps. Professionals are trained to keep the client within the limits of all kind of aggressive acts: the earlier controlled and swallowed violence of a neurotic client, the hasting or explosive violence of a psychotic client and the inwardly directed aggression of the depressed individual. This is true for all verbal aggression: shouting, yelling and reproaches. Therapists are less armed against physical violence. When a professional himself becomes a potential victim, the fear and uneasy feeling grows. This can lead to overestimation or underestimation of the degree of danger from the client.

Those two elements come essentially from the same reasons that the violent criminals also feel: fear, powerlessness and anger. The underestimation of the degree of danger posed by the client is then translated in a form of denial of reality and banalizing the signals.

The therapist starts to partially identify with the aggressor. When the degree of danger from the client is overestimated it is translated in an exaggerated form of his fear, and violent fantasies and the dramatization of his attitude and movements at the moment of his aggressive attack. In general this happens when the therapist is alone with the violent client and feels in an unsafe position. These two traps we also discover in the treatment of violent clients. The overestimation of the danger will go hand in hand with the rejection or punishment, the underestimation with a too great understanding of the therapist.

It is inevitable that therapist construct a close team to be able to work with dangerous criminals. Otherwise there is the danger that the whole team will fall into another trap: the one of sympathizing with the violent client. This means that the client will idealize one part of the team while the other part will get all his hostility. It is his way to divide the team. As long as this gap exists it will be very difficult to show the client the elements that fit his degree of dangerosity. It will become very difficult to ask deeper questions about the masquerade of deep inner pain of the client.

Unlike aggressive offenders who project their frustrations onto adults, child killers project their fear and anger at children. For a therapist it is less dangerous to work with child killers than to work with other kinds of violent murderers. If the tensions of the treatment become too heavy, the offender will eventually hideaway in his pervert fantasies where he kills children, but it is very unlikely that he will expose his anger towards the professional. He has feared adults since he was a child.

It isn't very clear exactly why he chooses children. It is very probable that he has been emotionally killed by sexual abuse in his own childhood and. in fact they are cowards. They don't fear much retaliation from a child and especially not verbal violence that would denigrate and humiliate them. With adult victims it is much more evident, not only could they physically defend themselves, they can also defend themselves verbally and these are two reasons why he chooses the way with the less restraints. It is also possible that criminals who never choose only children, were victims of physical violence in their childhood or they have only been the witnesses of extreme violence in the family or neighborhood. A deep investigation will show the differences. It is not only important to know this, it is especially necessary for prevention and to adapt treatment for each different kind of offender. When the typology or the profile of the criminal is clearly defined it makes the right treatment easier to define too.

Circles of abuse

There are several circles in which these kinds of crimes develop.

The first one is the continual circle in which the offender develops the pre-crime-thinking. This stage evaluates easily into repeated fantasy thinking. From that point the offender searches for a goal and once focused on this goal he starts looking for a target that he will groom and finally isolate. Then he commits his crime. This crime will strengthen his fantasies because he will copy what happened in his future fantasies. Then the offender is back at the point of departure with his pre-crime-thinking pattern and repeated fantasies: the circle is complete.

Another circle is the 'short cycle' one: the offender develops the pre-crime-thinking but also starts to behave and think as it. He will behave annoyingly and look for trouble in his environment. He hopes to be rejected by others. This helps him to fall into the right mood to take his next step in the circle. The inhibitions fail, unless he learned how to maintain them. In the next step he keeps his finger to the trigger and looks for excuses to justify his behavior. The mill of fantasies starts turning, fuelled by all kinds of sexual desires. The offender begins his search for a victim, grooms it, isolates it and then commits the crime. He will then again join this experience to his fantasies and again the cycle is complete.

A third circle starts with the pre-crime-thinking and the thereto linked behavior. Here too the inner brakes fall away. With his finger to the trigger he then makes a step from fantasy to reality. He pushes his feelings of guilt away, his fantasies are fuelled. He looks for a victim, isolates it, commits his crime and adds the facts to his fantasies. But this kind of criminal becomes frightened after his crime. The feelings of guilt reappear immediately after committing his crime. He has to make them go away because otherwise he cannot live with himself anymore. But here too we see that he will end up where he started: when his feeling of guilt fades away, he starts his cycle from the beginning again.

Fantasies can be very intensive but also volatile. This makes it that the offender can only enjoy his fantasies for a short period of time. After a while the recollection disappears slowly and he will be forced to commit a crime in reality again to reload it.

Unfortunately this also is the case for child killers who enjoyed this part of the fantasy and who join this killing to their fantasy. They too feel the need to commit a new crime in reality whereon they can live again for a while. In stress related situations the paedosexual will run away into his fantasies until he makes a new move in reality.

CHAPTER 3

Victimology

What is victimology?

Victimology is a new development in the criminological research area. It dates from after the Second World War and this new element was first used on war victims.

Until then there was only attention for the role of the criminal in a crime. The role of the criminal was clear. His rights and duties were clearly described (for instance: the right to an attorney), he formed the subject of expertise and sanctions and finally the criminal was guided to reintegrate in society. For victims . . . there was almost nothing.

More and more our authorities give attention to the victims. What role did the victim play in the crime? What is the psychological profile of the victim? Are there different types of victims? Is it possible to make a victim profile? What can the typology of a victim say of the offender? The relationship between offender and victim is also examined. This knowledge can be added to the already existing knowledge of crime and to help solve crimes and offences.

Of course we need more research in this area of criminology. Not only courage and perseverance, but also financial support is needed to expand this area of criminology. Belgium and large parts of Europe are not ready to make this commitment. We see here in Europe that experts try to develop their knowledge in the US or in England where the research is more actively encouraged than on the continent, and where they can count on support and encouragement.

To gain a better understanding of a crime, the victimologist will divide the crime into different parts. He will gather all the elements to profile both the criminal and the victim, then he will analyze the dynamics of the crime.

The dynamics of a crime.

If we take, for instance, a violent crime with a deadly outcome that took place in the middle of a busy city, we can deduce immediately some elements about the criminal and the victim.

The criminal is taking a considerable amount of risks to be captured or recognized. He doesn't care about eventual witnesses; he leaves traces behind him, this points to an impulsive type of offender.

As we saw before, we can consider this criminal type in general as being of moderate intelligence, socially inadequate and immature, probably no regular job and sexually incompetent. It is someone who has no clear picture of his 'sexual nature'. One can say that the impulsive type is ignorant about sexual events and maybe he is even disgusted by sexuality. He comes from a family with a very authoritarian father from whose example he copies. The offender feels fear when committing his crime and very probably attacks under the influence of alcohol. After committing his crime he has passed the climax of his stress and just let go of the idea. He forgets all about it. It is not something that will possess his mind to refine or use as a new hang up for his fantasies. For this offender, it happened, it released his stress and that is it. The crime is committed in an urge and that urge already disappears some minutes after the act. The crime will have no influence on his life style in any way. He continues to live where he always lived; if in some way he has to pass the crime scene to visit someone, he will not make the effort to take another way.

We also know of that criminal profile that the type of victim has little importance. In this case the victim is only a person that is 'in the wrong place at the wrong time." It might seem unimportant at first, but it is extremely important to catalogue this offender. He is the kind of criminal that thinks in an obsessive and compulsive way. His thinking world and his reality are primitive. His thoughts at the moment of the crime are desperate and confused. The crime scene and the circumstances of the crime in general give the impression that the criminal attacked very suddenly without a clear plan. The crime scene projects great disorder and gives spontaneous, symbolic and unplanned reflexions.

The victim can be known to the offender, but in general age, sex or looks have no importance for the criminal. Imagine that the criminal, in his search for a victim, knocks at every front door in his neighborhood, then the chances are very real that the first person that opens the door will become his victim.

This kind of criminal kills instantly to gain instant control. He cannot take the risk that the victim gets the upper hand. He approaches the victim from the back and overwhelms it, or he kills the victim instantly. The unexpected violent attack comes as a complete surprise for the victim. It is often someone who is busy with his daily activities at the moment of the attack.

The impulsive offender often depersonalizes and dehumanizes his victim. Particular parts of the body get extra violent attention. The use of more violence than necessary to kill the victim, goes with the destruction of the face. Herewith the offender unconsciously wants to destroy the human aspect of the victim. It is possible that the victim knew the criminal or the victim resembled by coincidence someone who inflicted psychological pain in the past to the criminal.

Some impulsive criminals wear a mask or handcuff and cover the face of the victim. They talk little or not at all during the crime and if they do, they threaten or give orders.

When proof of sadistic sexual violence is found on the victim, we can almost be sure that those were inflicted after death. An impulsive criminal isn't really focused on torturing someone. He gains his sexual pleasure from the mutilation of the body while the victim isn't playing a role in this. Unlike the methodical type who gets incredibly aroused by seeing the fear in the eyes of the victim while he tortures her.

Generally the scene of the murder and the scene where the body is found are the same when it concerns an impulsive type of killer. He doesn't even try to move the body or to conceal it. Sometimes the killer puts the body or body parts in a specific position that has only a special symbolic importance to him. Therefore it is very important that nothing is touched or displaced at the crime scene before precise pictures and/or films have been made. These elements have to be examined extensively. Each crime tells a story, the story of the criminal. One can read the state of mind of the offender in the crimes he commits. We can also see if it is anger motivated or if it is orchestrated pleasure. The offender doesn't necessary have to be angry at the moment of his act of murder. He can easily kill because it fits at that very moment into his fantasies. At the crime scene we often find footprints and fingerprints. Usually the impulsive criminal uses a weapon he finds on the spot. This can be a piece of rope, a heavy stone or rock or he can decide eventually to drown the victim in a nearby ditch or lake. Very often the weapon is found in the immediate surrounding of the victim. It is very important to read the story of the impulsive type in every element in and around the victim.

In the case of a methodical type we have to work the opposite way: first we have to find the murderer to be able to locate the victim. Because of the fact that the methodical type is conscious that traces can lead to his capture, he will spend an important amount of time in hiding the body of his victims. This thus becomes a very serious part of his fantasy and planning system. I here fore remind the reader of John's story and the description of that type in Chapter II

Everything depends on, if arrested, the criminal agrees to show where he has hidden the body. This type is very intelligent and socially well adapted. He is well dressed and usually has an important social position. He also is sexually competent. Research showed that the father of the methodical type also had a steady job and life. But the childhood of such offenders often shows that it is marked by inconsequence's and instability. What had been allowed one day is forbidden the other day and he was severely punished for the same wrongdoing.

During his crime the offender has everything under control. He has no fear and knows exactly what he is going to do. Generally he uses more alcohol than the impulsive type before beginning his crime. During the crime he is very tense, which often leads to temporary impotence. This doesn't mean that he does not commit sexual acts; on the contrary, he gains sexual pleasure out of the domination and demonstration of power over the victim.

This type of criminal is often married and is above suspicion. He is mobile and is able to travel hundreds of kilometers to find a victim. He follows the investigation later in the media. It continues to arouse him. If he suspects that the investigation is coming in his direction, he moves and changes jobs. He plans his crime and takes care that there is no link between him and the victim. The criminal and the victim do not or hardly know each other.

In contrast to the impulsive type this man wants that its victim has a human face. Its victim is for him no object but a human being whom he can humiliate and abuse. He thus controls the conversation between him and the victim and he deliberately explains to the victim what he is going to do. The fear in the eyes of his victim arouses him. If the victim can manage to give the impression that he is not intimidated or afraid of the offender then he has a chance of survival.

If this offender proceeds to assassination, one can see that in the whole picture everything is controlled. This type of criminal inflicts his aggressive actions before he kills his victim. The weapon of assassination is never retrieved on the spot. As said previously the offender moves its victim and he also carefully covers all his tracks. He refined his techniques to approach his victim; this also has to fulfill certain conditions that fit his fantasies even if it is a child. In general children have to look 'pure', 'like an angel' and 'innocent'.

It takes much longer to capture a methodical type of criminal than an impulsive one. The consequences are that the methodical type can have more victims than the impulsive one. In general these types of crimes are intra-racial. Seldom will a colored criminal choose a white victim and only few cases are known whereby a white offender took a black victim. The reason could be that the offender has a mother profile in his mind: a mother from whom he had missed the protection and love he needed so much.

Analysis of the offender profile.

Analysis of the file

To get a better insight into the way killers operate and what their backgrounds and motivations are, we should gather together all the unsolved cases of child disappearance and child murder. I know it is a tremendous amount of work and we need to collect it from all over the world. We have now seen how these criminals function and as a collector of stamps, he will travel all over that world to find exactly the stamp/victim he wants. We also saw how Johnny travelled and how John lived for 18 months in the U.S. He told me he had killed children there. But cooperation seems to be so difficult between countries. This lack of cooperation lacks humanity. While politicians and police departments discuss what is possible and what is not, parents are desperately seeking their children. Some of them for over twenty years!

In Europe too, hundreds of parents are waiting for news about a family member. Not only should the cold cases be re-examined but also the solved cases from which the criminals have been arrested and who have confessed to their crimes should be put back on the table. This is very important not only to better understand how these crimes are committed but also to link already convicted prisoners to unsolved cases. It is evident that, an aggressive, violent and fantasy loaded criminal who is arrested at the age of 45 for one crime, that this is not at his first crime at that age. This kind of criminal has a career in killing and it starts around the age of 29. It is also evident that someone who is arrested for one crime, will not spontaneously admit to previous ones. I'll give an example that everybody can understand. Imagine that you are in a jewellery store and you are delighted with one particular diamond ring. The shopkeeper is busy with another client. You are waiting and he didn't even bother to say 'hello' to you. Fifteen minutes pass by. The shopkeeper is laughing with the other customer, they don't seem to notice you. You begin to feel angry. Who do they think they are? You are as good as a customer as the other woman. Twenty five minutes later, you are still there ... waiting. The shopkeeper takes the woman to a corner of the shop.

He can not see you from where he stands. You think: "I'll take the ring. It is his fault. He made me wait for so long." You put it into your shoe. Another ten minutes go by and you are still waiting because you just cannot walk out like this. That would be suspicious. You want to ask him about the earrings. He is not looking at you at all. You take the earrings and put them into your pocket. Another ten minutes pass and you are now going to steal the necklace that matches the earrings and the ring. At that point the shopkeeper sees what you are doing. He calls the police and they stop you. What are you going to do? You cannot deny the necklace because it has been seen and the shopkeeper saw where you put it. So you will do whatever you can to focus on the necklace and to divert the attention from a further search. The last thing you will want to do is to say: "Ho! You ain't seen anything yet! Look what I hid in my shoes, and look what I had in my pocket! . . ."

Killers react the same way. They have no intention of telling you everything, so why should they do it?

Conversations with killers.

To gain an insight into the mind of killers and to be able to understand why and how they commit crimes it is very important to talk to them in prison. You have to be armed with a very detailed list of questions. Such conversations can only take place in an atmosphere of confidence and understanding which isn't the same as showing approval for the crime. In the right conditions we can obtain a lot of information that helps in refining the art of profiling. With this information we can start to work on the cold cases.

It is absolutely necessary that investigators are trained for this specific task. I personally have experienced the sense of horror and abomination when a killer is giving specific details of his crime. A lot of feelings are aroused when working with them and sometimes investigators do not know exactly how to deal with these confused feelings. We can never forget that the best profilers are the criminals themselves. They live as survivors which gives them the opportunity to observe more details than we do. Since their childhood they are trained to recognize feelings and body languages of others to determine if they are in danger or not. Is daddy angry? Will he hit mummy? Is mummy tired? Will she lock me in the basement? Is the neighbor having that strange desiring glow in his eyes? These killers know exactly what someone is thinking by observing their body language. It speaks for itself that they permanently observe the body language of their investigators. There is no sense questioning a killer with your arms crossed. The message? 'That investigator wants to know things from me but he is sure that I would know something about him, that's why he crosses his arms in front of his body.' This does not engender feelings of confidence. The criminal will also play with your feelings and reactions. He will shock you with details: blood, screaming victims ... He will try to get you upset, angry, disgusted. Once he succeeds in this, the questioning is over. He is in control of the situation not you and that is the worst scenario possible. So it is imperative that the professional completely controls his own body language and the body language of the killer.

No passion for murderers.

Unfortunately it sometimes happens that the investigator gets emotionally involved in the life and the feelings of dangerous criminals, but it is seldom.

As a child and even as an adolescent these offenders almost all had a very difficult time. Some of the caretakers and therapists want to be the saviors, the rescuers of these lost souls. I will be very clear in this: it is most unlikely that these people can be 'rescued'. It is possible that they really want to be helped from the bottom of their hearts, but their whole life has been built on instability and insecurity that it is impossible that we can build on this. Everything will slide away on such poor ground. Several cases are known of women who felt the urge and the call to 'rescue' murderers. For most of them this venture becomes fatal. For some of the killers manifestations have been organized to 'give them a chance'. It is a very charitable initiative, because the death penalty has no effect whatsoever on criminals of this kind, but there is a trap. Some active members of this school of thought do not want to admit that the 'sweet man' on death row is a real killer. It is indeed so that most killers can be very charming when they are in a closed system such as a prison. They function quite well in this controlled and easy way of living. There are no temptations and they have strict and many rules which they cannot handle in real life and in freedom. For them this freedom is just too much because they never learned to respect limits and others. For them life outside is without limits in the real sense of the word. They will allow themselves everything they want. For such criminals life in a good restricted way is more livable than outside. Oh, sure, they want to get out of prison but they just cannot live there. While they are in a closed system, they can be very nice. Many caretakers are surprised to see that they are such sweet, nice, obliging people. Some of these social workers just don't seem to realize that many killers and particularly child killers are the best manipulators on earth. It even happens that a 'rescuing angel' marries this sweet, nice man in prison. When the offender is released after many years of prison and he didn't have serious treatment for his problems and deviant behavior, we have seen that some of them kill their 'angel' after a while. Because, the criminal is still what he is: a killer.

Despite the fact that some individuals believe they are able to change a murderer and to convert him to a better life, it will not work. Murderers need long and intensive treatment to get some kind of stable ground beneath their feet instead of an ever sucking marsh.

Empathize with the pain and the suffering of the murderer is allowed, sympathizing is not.

Minimize or deny the fact is out of the question. Those who feel called to be part of a strictly structured team to work on this problem have to remember only one thing: only the truth in its purest form is the basis for constructive work. Expectation is better not to be too high.

It is worth working on this tremendous painful problem. It stays incomprehensible that some authorities authorize the release of a child killer without any form of treatment or control. We now know the consequences of these irresponsible decisions.

Child killers make a lot of victims.

I am convinced that an unknown amount of child killers are in prison for only one child murder, namely the solved case, but in fact they killed several children.

Research in the United States showed that child killers do not start to kill at the age of fifty. They start much earlier. The paranoiac peak appears around the age of twenty-four. At that age they already have heavy and serious violent fantasies. And most of them have already several crimes on their conscience, generally the killing starts around the age of twenty-nine. This means that a criminal who is arrested at the age of fifty for murder, this is not his first crime. Early or late, he had to run against the wall; unfortunately that mostly happens much too late. He will be confused after his first crime and he will probably not lose too much time in erasing all tracks, but once he had committed his second crime he had already learned a lot, especially if he is not bothered by the police he will imagine that he is outsmarting them. When he has past his peak he is likely to become careless, unwittingly leaving traces behind, believing he is smarter than the police and thus intangible.

Many parents of missing children have to live with the unsolved case of the disappearance of their child. When we study precisely the Modus Operandi in each child murder separately we would be able to see a certain amount of unsolved cases in another perspective. We would be able to compare cases and look for the same Modus Operandi and signatures. I am convinced that we would be able to solve a lot of cold cases.

We have few precise numbers in Europe, some say that approximately four thousand children and youngsters disappear per year. This figure doesn't take in account the runaway children, but only disappearances within a criminal pattern. There are no precise figures because the law on underage children forbids the circulation of this information. Four thousand children per year means forty thousand in ten years, this is a huge number and I am sure that there are many more. This also means that forty thousand families live in fear and uncertainty for their children!

The development of the internet makes it even more urgent to react and to adapt the laws in every country of the world. It always amazed me that in some cases the law can be changed in twenty-four hours, but if it concerns children it takes an average of seven years!. Recently the tobacco industry in Belgium wanted to lower the price of cigarettes, it took an amazing twelve hours to forbid this by law although there was no law that could forbid it at first. The same happened some years ago concerning Chiquita bananas. Only twenty-four hours to change the law for the sale of bananas!! For children it takes many years. Did you know that the laws to protect children have only existed since 1965? And did you know that the law to protect animals dates from 1864! It took a hundred years to realize that children too had the right to protection and still the laws are not applied. There is no reason for panic, but we absolutely need to do everything we can to protect children, but every time I knocked on doors for financial aid as well as professional help, I was stunned by the lack of interest.

Once at a conference in Washington D.C., I bought a wonderful sticker: "A world of wanted children would make a world of difference"! This is so true!

Analysis of Victimology

People often get upset when they hear that the victim too plays a role in a crime, but unfortunately this is the case. It is evident that it is not the choice of the victim to be chosen as a victim, but it is important to look at the elements that made that person a victim. We can determine that some people become the victim several times in the same sort of crime. Some women are raped at different times in their life, while this never happens to others. There are some men who are the victims of assault while it never happens to others. It is also often the same children who become the victim of violence or rape and other children are never disturbed. Here in the environment, the circumstances and the lifestyle of the victim as well as the offender can play an important role. It seldom happens that a rich person attacks another rich person in the street.

The big difference in a crime is that the criminal makes a choice to attack someone and he also makes the choice of who the victim will be, while the victim has no choice whatsoever. The offender chooses, the victim is chosen. The offender plays an active role in the attack, the victim plays a passive role in the crime. But nevertheless the crime took place and we have to examine why the criminal chose that particular victim. This will help us develop better prevention for the future.

It is thus important to gain as much information as possible about the victim. How does this person live? Whom does she encounter? Where does she work? Did she have conflicts in the past with others? At what time did the crime occur? What were the weather conditions? Where did the crime take place?

CHAPTER 4

Prevention and Victim Aid

How can we protect ourselves?

How can we protect ourselves and avoid becoming the victim of a violent crime? A profound study of criminals gives us some clues. Although of course it is very difficult to stay reasonable and under control when we are chosen as a victim, I will give some advice.

It is important to break the fantasies of the criminal. In his fantasy everything about his crime goes precisely the way he planned his crime. In reality this plan can be profoundly shaken up when the victim doesn't react in the way the criminal had in mind. He is not prepared for this unforeseen change and it is possible that he will run away. It can depend on very small details to get him off balance. It all depends on the type of criminal. If it is an offender who gets a kick out of dependency and subservience, and is then confronted with a victim who is brutal and assertive, then the victim has a good chance of escaping A reaction as 'Ok, let's rent a room where we both can find what we seek', this response, full of confidence can also scare the hell out of the offender. This is not what he planned. He doesn't want to have 'peace and quiet. He will commit his act now, immediately and if possible with a submissive victim, not with a victim that gives the orders herself and who has total control over the situation. Only he is allowed to have control and he is not expecting such a reaction. What he DID expect was resistance and struggle. Therefore he will do whatever is in his power to avoid resistance from the victim. Physical resistance is thus dangerous. It can bring the criminal into a state of panic and as a consequence he can kill the victim. When a victim behaves as if its life isn't worth a penny, it will confuse the offender completely, much more than physical resistance. Some criminals get a kick from physical resistance. It is the category that chooses victims because they know that she is physically incapable of defending herself, most of the time these victims are small, thin and fragile.

The most important step is to not behave as a victim. This means that you have to try to avoid remote and isolated areas. If you have no choice, then walk resolutely with your head up as if you are walking in a busy city street. As soon as you have the feeling that you are being followed by someone, don't walk faster but start walking slower. The courageous amongst us can even turn back to the offender to ask what time it is for instance and then start walking again. Herewith his fantasies are badly damaged, these unexpected circumstances do not fit into what he had in mind. He will most probably murmur something and run away. When indeed he does walk away one will never know if he was trying something, but at least you avoided the risk of getting in trouble.

Recently I saw a movie wherein a young woman is assaulted by an exhibitionist. When the offender suddenly showed himself naked to the woman, he didn't get the reaction he wished for. On the contrary, the woman looked closely at the naked body part and said coldly: "Hmmm, it looks like a penis but much smaller". The aggressor had to run away. If he had seen a woman in shock and frightened he would have fulfilled his fantasy. He wasn't expecting an assertive reaction.

But what to do when the victim is not the hero kind of type? And what if she is unable to react in this confident way? She should avoid eye contact with the offender if possible. He can read in your eyes everything he needs to know. Fear, horror, uncertainty and helplessness lie in the look. Report what happened to the police. These elements can be important in the future.

Prevention for children.

For children the prevention is obviously different. Children are raised with the rule that they have to obey the orders of adults. For a child every adult is an authority. Not only physically but also mentally a child can not stand up to adults. It would be good to redirect the education of children to make them more assertive.

For a child the visual aspect is important. In that option I wrote a play with Johan Waegeman, a teacher. 'Fragile but not Defenseless' is a play for adults as well as children. It is made in six blocks. Each block is a finished scenario and a mixture of choreography, music and conversations. The parts are played by adults and children. Schools can ask for one, three or all of the blocks. A funny kangaroo runs through the play as a bound between the different blocks. The kangaroo narrates and explains what is going on, without moralizing. In his bag are hundreds of little pieces of paper with the secrets of children written on them. He reads some of them, between two chapters. He asks himself aloud which letters should stay a secret and which are not. One of the blocks starts with a grooming scene. Dance and music accompanies the piece. The accent lies on the visual and auditive aspects. The audience is confronted with a little girl who is sexually abused by her uncle. Her friends remark that she is behaving strangely and they tell it to their teacher.

In the second block the rights of children are shown. Since 1994 children have had a new right in Belgium, but they don't even know it. If nobody shows them what their rights are, how could they ever know? It is not the offender that will tell them. The right to be heard by a judge is very important. It implicates that a child itself can ask the judge to be heard not only in sexual abuse but also in situations where the child is in trouble, for instance in a divorce. A nice judge is presented in the next chapter and he takes the time to listen to the child and what it wants. Together they discuss what should happen to the child sex offender in the play. Sometimes the offender is the father of the child and that child does not want its daddy to end up in prison. It only wants the abuse to stop. It wants 'it' to stop. A child is very loyal and forgiving but can perfectly say what it wants when it comes to an appropriate measure for the offender.

In yet another chapter we can see how a therapy goes with a child sex offender. There is no question of repression or violence. In an atmosphere of trust and understanding the actor-therapist explores the deeper motivation and the consequences of the crime and the play shows also how the offender can learn to control his impulses.

We know that other paedosexuals come watch that theatre. They see themselves reflected in the play and it should help them to seek professional treatment.

There are no shocking facts in this scenario. Maybe some of the statements of children can worry some adults for instance when we see them in a scene of group therapy together with other sexually abused children. But it is reality and our experience showed us that children can manage reality very well. What children do not manage is hypocrisy and lies. It confuses them and makes them afraid.

We also treat the prevention of sexual crimes. We explain to children what they can do when they are approached by adults with bad intentions. It is important for a child to know that it is not alone in this. Many children are victims of sexual abuse. The purpose of this play is to remove the child from its isolation. Very often we hear that children are convinced that they are the only children in the world to whom this happens. Deep shame and embarrassment prevents them from talking about it with someone. The play is an indication for the child who suffers from that fear, confusion and pain.

Parents from whom their children are never confronted with these problems will probably be worried when they watch the play. I want to reassure them. The theatre is made in such a way that each child, irrespective of the fact whether it is sexually abused or not, will be warned in a very preventive manner. They learn a lot but they will not have the feeling that life is dangerous.

Teaching a child to say 'no' when it is touched in an indecent way is important. The whole theatre shows ways in which children can do that and what the reaction could be of people who want to help them. The theatre does not only send out messages to children but also to judges and therapists to show how they could react and act. Very often judges do not know how to deal with this embarrassing problem and they are not trained to talk to an abused child. The play also shows teachers and caretakers what to do with a child they suspect of being sexually abused. We hope they find the courage and the responsibility to do something to protect the children. Maybe they will find a way to make a school project based on the theatre to make it easier for children to talk about any eventual abuse.

I want to make clear with this project that we all have responsibilities to take when it comes to child abuse in any form. We: the parents, teachers, social workers, policemen, magistrates, neighbors ... every adult. This doesn't mean that there are child sex offenders waiting for children at every corner of the street or that children are in a permanent danger. A child should not to be educated in an atmosphere of paranoia and fear. We can make children a little bit more confident with dangers in our society that are not always visible. It is natural to show children the dangers of the street, to teach them to not cross a street when the lights are red, to not ride their bicycles without a light ... it must be as natural to teach them the other dangers.

Parents should teach their children a code word, or a password that only they and the closest family know. When someone comes to pick up the child at school, the child can ask for the password. If the person cannot give it, then the child should know what to do: not go with that person and contact an adult to tell what is going on. If, for instance, you cannot pick up your son at school in time, you can ask a colleague to do it for you. You can then give the password to him or her. It is important to change it regularly. Code words become normal after a while especially when given to others. So the child also needs to know that it may not give this password to someone else and that this is a good secret that should be kept secret with the parents only. Children are very fond of secrets. It seems like a game with the parents. But the parent has to explain what the difference is between a 'good' secret and a 'bad' secret because if anyone knows what children think about 'secrets' it is surely the child sex offenders. They abuse that again.

Someone with bad intention will very quickly go off his idea when confronted with a child that asks for a code. Paedosexuals often use false excuses to trap a child: "your mother has had an accident, I have to take you to the hospital." This confuses children and therefore they have to be made aware of these dangers.

I also see that a considerable amount of people are nonchalant with the safety of their children. The responsibility for the safety of children lies with the parents in the first place. They know how their children react and what their attitudes and habits are. It should alert parents when the behavior of their child changes drastically. A sudden change can have different reasons. But parents need to know that one of these reasons can be sexual abuse.

Patience and lots of empathy help the child to talk about what happened. In no way should the child be accused or feel embarrassed about what adults did to them. Nor is it permitted to minimize the facts or to deny the facts.

But much more important than the prevention plans for children, are the prevention plans for adults. Above all, people, they are the ones that are supposed to know the law and to know that touching a child in an indecent way is a crime. All adults know that sexually abusing a child is damaging for its development and it is simply not done. There is that stupid excuse that in 'some cultures' it is a must or it is normal. The most used example of that, is that in Egypt fathers had the right to 'introduce' their daughters and mothers had the duty to 'initiate' their sons. This is all a lie. Incest was indeed very common but especially for heritage reasons. To keep the richness in the families. Anthropological research has proven that in the most primitive cultures in New-Guinea and Central America, incest and child sexual abuse are condemned by the whole tribe. It is condemned all over the world as a repulsive act. I often see the subject discussed on the internet and often I am attacked for my point of view. Don't think I didn't reflect on all of this. When one works with child sex offenders alone, one starts to believe them after six months. I can understand that professionals who work only with child sex offenders, start to empathize too much because there is no challenge from the opposite side: the victim. At times I really was taken with the pitiful story of the offender. I started wondering if I myself had a problem with not accepting sex between an adult and a child. Offenders tell you how beautiful it all is and how the child liked it and asked for it. 'Who am I to say anything to the contrary' I thought. I've never been the victim of child abuse. 'Maybe indeed children like this?' But because I work with both parties: offenders and victims, I also see the suffering and the damage done to a child. In my whole career of twenty years I only saw one girl, who was a woman when I spoke to her, who said that in fact she didn't suffer from the child abuse in her life.

"It was something", she said, "That shouldn't have happened, but I did not suffer from it." She is the only victim like this that I know. I want to make clear that whoever you are as a reader, you don't have to feel guilty if the sexual abuse in your life didn't affect you. It is alright. But most of the victims had a lifetime of trouble and pain and for these people we absolutely need to direct the prevention campaigns towards the adults and not towards the children. It is not up to children to protect themselves. It is up to us, as adults, to take responsibility for their safety.

Therefore I want to see large advertising boards in the streets and warnings on television directed at the adult who has bad things in mind. Don't worry, it doesn't have to be shocking. It is enough to show a man with a child on a sofa. The man caresses the hair of the child while they are watching a movie. The slogan could be: 'if you caress your child, is it for you or for her?' Someone with no bad intentions will not be offended. It is obvious: 'if I caress my child, I do it for my child.' Those who do feel offended should go to see a professional. Child sex abuse happens in secret. Always! The criminal feels free and not observed. We could change that with clear messages visible for all of us. Child sex offenders have to know that they are observed and that society will never accept their abusive behavior towards the weakest of society.

It is not up to a child to say 'no' to an adult. It is up to the adult to say 'no'.

Therapy: Letting go of the role of victim.

What if a child is indeed sexually abused? It is sad that a therapy which is meant to heal, often works stigmatizing. Most of the time the child is confirmed in its' victim role. It looks as if the abused child cannot have positive expectations again. We take their defense weapons, with which they could be able to fight for their healing, away beforehand. Many children I had in treatment, lost a lot of precious time with therapists who put too much accent on the aspect of the abuse. There are other aspects too. It is absolutely necessary to give a lot of attention to these aspects to heal the self esteem of a child. A child is so much more than abused! When only the damaged child is treated, the self esteem lowers even more. We then push the child deeper in its victim role. It is important to show the child all the positive aspects of its personality and to work with those elements which have been destroyed by the abuser.

Luckily the notion of the fact that the therapy has to be based on communication on both sides becomes clear. In the classical perception of therapy the patient can come one or two hours a week to talk about his problem. The psychiatrist or the psychologist only listens. Challenging the point of view of the victim or giving advice was not allowed. All the efforts had to come from the patient. The fact that the patient had hundreds of questions for which it tried to find the answers, seemed of underlying importance. But that is just what therapy is about: trying to find the answers to questions with which the patient is struggling with. It cannot do it alone. Therefore it is too confused and too manipulated by the offender. It is to compare with someone who comes to see a doctor and says: 'Doctor, I am suffering from permanent headaches" and the doctor answers: "What do you think it could be?" Let's be realistic, if you are confronted with such a reaction, you just go and look for another doctor to give you the answer. Otherwise you could have done the studies of a doctor yourself. Yes, then you would have been able to give advice and diagnostics for your own diseases. Why then is it asked from a victim of sexual abuse? Why does that victim have to be a psychiatrist to be able to find the answers to its' own problems?

For the treatment of child sex offenders it is the same. How many times have I heard: "But why am I like this? I would so much to be like everyone else. Why am I unable to control my impulses? And how do I have to learn that?"

Can you imagine me saying: "Why do you think you are like that?"
Isn't it better and more reasonable to go with the client and find out together? Many patients leave their session with their psychiatrist with more questions than when they came in. This is an unhealthy situation. Many professionals have formed the idea that the patient will find the answers once the questions arise in their minds. They don't seem to realize that if the

patients have already found the answers, they could be the wrong ones, or answers that confused them even more. It is also probable that the patient does not find the answers and lives a lifetime with all the questions.

Many children suffer from the idea that they are lost for society once they are stigmatized as a 'sexually abused child'. A fourteen year old girl went weekly to see her psychiatrist for more than a year. She was sexually molested from her fourth year till her tenth by a family friend. But a year later she was still bedwetting and sometimes she even came home from school with her underwear wet. She still had nightmares and anger attacks. Her mother was desperate. For three hours I talked to the girl. I tried to form an idea of what she felt and what she wanted. At the end of our conversation I said: "Look, you have two options. You stay in the role of a victim wherein you obviously do not feel good, and you try with me to get to the bottom of why all this has happened to you, or you draw a line over the past and start working on your future. You are fourteen years old, with a whole life waiting for you. A life that wants to embrace you with open arms. You have to run to it. If you are not ready to go, I am willing to help you to bridge this first period. Together we will seek for the why's, and as soon as you feel you are ready for that life, I let you go."

To support a client in his role of a victim works paralyzing and keeps the dependency in score. It is all about the retrieval of the need of the victim, give support and advice and herein strengthen the will for life of the victim. The victim only wants to avoid that he or she becomes a victim again in the future and it also wants to understand why it has been a victim. Offenders can almost blindly pick out a potential victim. This is no reproach to the victim, far from this, but only a warning that the person in question has to undertake something to avoid becoming a victim again in the future. Stand up for yourself, daring to say 'no', being strong and sure of yourself are elements that will discourage an offender.

Victims need an example of other victims who have overcome this problem and made it in life. It gives them hope that they too can succeed if they see how others managed step by step to get their life back together. You also show the victim how their life can be. Until now the media only shows us people that still are victims and who do not succeed in getting out of that role, while so many do succeed and have a wonderful life!

The same applies to offenders of violent acts. They too need to have an example of criminals that succeeded in getting out of these destructive cycles and who are able to testify that he feels good in his skin since he left the misery behind him. This kind of testimony would help to motivate other offenders to do something about their problems so they can be reintegrated into society again as a full member.

Working at a positive self image is the most important goal of every therapy, it can take a long time, but with encouragement, understanding, appreciation, good will and patience everybody can reach that goal. Even people who think that they are lost and who comfort themselves in self pity. A sex offender is also much more than just a sex offender.

On the other hand they will seldom seek professional help themselves. There are different reasons for this. The most common reason is that they think they have no problem. Society has a problem with sex between an adult and a child, not them. Another reason is that they are in a difficult situation if they really want to stop abusing children. When they go to the police to talk about their problem, there is a big chance that they will be arrested for previous assaults. When they go talk to a psychiatrist he can report it to the police. Anyway, most of the untrained professionals treat criminals as victims, which is very dangerous. Criminals are what they are: criminals. They choose to be a criminal and to commit criminal acts. The victim did not choose to be a victim. He or she has been chosen. A victim chooses to look for help. A criminal has to be pushed to accept treatment. A victim has every reason to tell the truth when it wants to be helped. A criminal has every reason not to tell the truth. He has no reason whatsoever to tell what is really going on in his mind. It is thus up to the professional to know as much as possible about criminals and how they think and act. Criminals have to be challenged and defied to make them talk. They have to feel that you know that they are lying and they also have to feel that they can trust you. Criminals will never trust anyone who they feel doesn't know enough about their subject. They will start the manipulation and domination right away, and very soon the professional feels sorry for them.

CONCLUSIONS

Myths about child sex offences.

This book has tried to demystify and take the edge off certain myths, wrong ideas, unfounded convictions and preconceptions about child sexual abuse.

Convictions as there are 'he is only interested in little girls' or 'he has a preference for boys' or 'he would never touch his own children' are completely unfounded. The child sex offender can express a preference, but in fact it doesn't matter that much. He reduces children to objects. If he cannot find girls, he will find the same satisfaction in boys. He isn't in fact looking for sexual gratification, he is looking for sexual arousal which he extracts from domination and suppression of his victim. He will look for children he can catch and who are easy to dominate and manipulate. If his own children aren't 'properly' watched by his wife, he will abuse his own children. It is also wrong to think that an incest offender will only abuse his own children. They use their children because they are the easiest to approach. As soon as their own children are not longer 'available', they will start looking for other opportunities.

"He didn't hurt the child" or "He is such a nice man, he would never hurt a child" we often hear. Indeed they exist, the paedosexuals who do not physically hurt children, but who says that this will always be the case? And who can guarantee that the children are not emotionally hurt and damaged? You can turn it the way you want but paedosexual acts are traumatic experiences for children. Everybody has the right to respect the physical integrity. If you want physical intimacy with someone, you can choose yourself. A child is not able to decide that. A child lives its' sexuality in his own immature way and cannot calculate what sexual intercourse with an adult can have as implications for the future. Nobody has the right to impose in a sexual way on a child. It is a complete lie to think that a paedosexual loves children. He loves the child because that child can give him sexual gratification. His love for a child is not more than an excuse. If he really loved the child, he would respect it.

Then there is the very dangerous myth of untrustworthy children. It is indeed even more dangerous because in some cases children do lie and give false testimonies. Divorcing mothers and fathers cite the incest stories to avoid custody or visiting rights for the other partner. This is a very dangerous tendency.

It is not that difficult to know if a child speaks the truth or if it is lying. Children who tell the truth never lie about the bottom of the story. Sometimes they hide events because they are ashamed or because they cannot find the right words. Sometimes they lie to protect a family member. Sometimes they lie because they are frightened to death because they have been threatened. 2 % of the stories children tell to the police or professionals are lies. We need to keep this in mind because it is an incredible drama if innocent person is sent to prison on the accusations of child sexual abuse.

A child of four years old, for instance, that tells a story like this:

"I was playing in my room. It was a Sunday, the second of June. My father came in and he touched me. He put his penis in my vagina . . ." is very probably lying. Children of that age do not give dates, months, days . . . simply because they don't know at that age. True stories go more like: "It was the day after the anniversary party of Cheryl. Daddy came to my room and hurt me . . ."

Children of four do not use words like: penis or vagina. They use childish words and anyway in their first statements they will turn around the real topic.

Breaking hellish circles.

We heard the story of John, of David, Johnny and so many others. There are many more Johnnys and Johns in prison and even more that live amongst us every day. There are thousands of adults who never found the courage to talk about what happened in their childhoods. They will never understand why someone did this to them when they were children. So many victims of victims with a ball of anger, hate and powerlessness deep inside them. One fears that one day they will take revenge by making new victims. These hellish circles that come back again and again have to be broken. We have to realize the consequences and take responsibility to protect children, so they won't become balls of hate and anger and they will not become offenders and make new victims in the next generations.

We thus urgently need specialized centers for the treatment of sexually abused children. If possible we have to involve the family. Only like this we can preserve the family structure which a child so desperate needs. Anyway the best person to heal and help a child is the mother. When the mother is well and professional guided, she is the best therapist a child can find. It is mostly the child's wish to keep the family structure intact. The existing centers are too overloaded and do not have enough resources. We need green telephone numbers where child sex offenders can ask for help to get out of their cycle of abuse before they re-offend. This is the only way to prevent that more victims are made.

It is therefore a sad fact that until now, such centers for child killers do not exist and thus an intensive treatment is not available.

Paedosexuality and paedosexual child killings are a specific section in the world of criminality. They need a special and adapted infrastructure within the penitentiary world where their anger and frustration should not have to be fuelled by death threats and aggravation from other prisoners.

The fact that they are housed together in extra safe parts of the prison gives opportunities to study them and to treat them.

Child killers cannot live in the free world. They need strict and clear structures. There is nothing to be gained in crying out for the death penalty. As I mentioned before, it will not frighten the candidate killers and the consequences for children will be worse than ever. Think about what the paedosexual will realize after committing his offence. This point of view has nothing to do with sympathy, on the contrary, it has everything to do with the naked reality of this problem.

Many people are upset when they hear me talk about specialized centers. But the question: 'where does the killer go after his prison sentence?' is not asked. Questions as: 'what will the killer do and feel when he is rejected overall?' or 'what shall he do after he is released to eliminate his frustrations?' are not considered either.

Killers don't think the way we do. They wouldn't be killers if they were thinking like us. It is no use to approach their crimes from a normal point of view. It is very important to know that policemen or therapists have to work with these people. Professionals need to be very alert for the violent fantasies of their clients. Often criminals suffer from his problems. Sometimes they don't. Violent criminals can talk about their fantasies if they have enough trust in their therapist and if they feel the therapist knows he had those fantasies. Unfortunately professional have this need to minimize the role of fantasies in violent crimes. They often tell their client: 'as long as they are fantasies, it isn't that bad.' And they continue to classify their clients as not dangerous. How can a professional then discover that the line between fantasy and reality has been crossed? Do we really always have to have victims before we react? As long as they are still fantasizing, we should examine them and analyze them so we can divert them or avoid them from acting out. Though, we know that as soon as fantasies have been transformed to reality the criminal will not talk about it anymore.

Most of our policemen approach those criminal acts from the point of view of a rational, clear thinking pattern. A murderer doesn't think rationally, let alone clearly. Why would a killer leave traces behind him, he must be crazy to do that, thinks the policeman. He doesn't reason from the mental system of someone who has just killed a child.

My attention reaches out to all the children and the adults that have been sexually abused in their childhood. I sincerely hope for them that they will realize one day that they are so much more than just a 'rape victim' and that for them, as anybody else, life is there for them. I want to encourage them to transform their trauma into positive energy. Do not give the offender the gratification of staying a victim for the rest of your life. I know, it shouldn't have happened in the first place, but believe me: there is no reason to say that this is the end of your life. Or that you will be damaged for ever. This is so not true.

My heart also bleeds for the parents of missing and murdered children. Without the courage and the perseverance of some parents, nothing would have changed. I think especially of Jean-Jacques Gerard whose eleven year old son had been killed. His boy would take a train that day and only had one stop to go to where his father was waiting for him. A young man of eighteen offered him 'some help' and Jean-Jacques' son never arrived at that station. Three days later the dead body of the little boy had been found. He was brutally raped and killed. Jean-Jacques was destroyed by grief and despair. Some months later he quit his job and started a psycho-analysis training. Then he decided to study psychology to become a psycho-analyst himself. Some years after the drama he opened his first centre for young violent youngster who are likely to become violent criminals in their lives. All these people were seriously maltreated and sexually abused in their childhood. They are all at the age where they have to make a choice: struggle through life or become a violent criminal. Jean-Jacques and his assistants help them to make the right choice. With a lot of patience, perseverance and creativity he leads his centre in the South of France. In this he has saved many many lives, not only of the criminals in the making, but especially of coming victims. His centre offers these youngsters a real home, something they have never known in their lives. Jean-Jacques is an example of how broken people can get up on their feet again. He shows how one can divert grief into something constructive. Each positive contribution, however difficult, provides a very important brick in the building of the tremendous structure of our society.

Although the problem is harrowing, I do not want to end this book in minor. In many countries the messages starts to pass through. Let us hope it continues and that we do everything in our power to stop this violence to children.

The body of Delphine, the little girl who disappeared in 1989 has finally been found in 2004. She was raped and killed by the serial killer Michel Fourniret. Arrested in Belgium, this French citizen admitted to over ten murders on children, as well as women and men. He abducted the child together with his wife, Monique, and his baby who slept in the back of the car. He told Delphine that he was looking for a doctor for his baby. Delphine who wanted them to show where her family doctor lived, stepped into the car. Immediately she was taken to France where Fourniret raped and killed her. He buried her body in the drive to his castle. For fifteen years, people walked and drove their cars over her body without knowing. At four meters from Delphine the body of Jeanne-Marie has been found. She was missing since 1987. The investigation in Belgium and France is still going on. Recently two new victims have been added to the list.

The anonymous killer of Eunice has still not been found.

The body of little Peter is still missing. The investigation is leading nowhere.

APPENDICES

I. *Information Sheets.*

Each time a child disappears or is found killed we should immediately gather as much information as possible. Details have to be noted. I managed to make an information sheet based on what the FBI uses as a standard model.

In case of disappearance:

1. Circumstances

Time of disappearance:
Day of disappearance:
Month of disappearance:
Year of disappearance:
Place of disappearance:
Description of the infrastructure of that area (roads, trains, bus stops, metro, highways . . .):
Pictures of the area where the child was last seen:
Pictures of the area where the child's body has been found:
Mapping:
Where was the child seen for the last time:

By whom:
What was the child doing:
What were the weather conditions at the time of the disappearance:
What did the child eat before disappearing:
Were there workers busy in the area (streets, electricity . . .)
Weather circumstances at the time of disappearance:

2. Victimology

Name:
Family name:
Age:
Sex:
Nationality:
Race:
Address:
Place of birth:
School:
Child illnesses:
Hospitals visited:
Family doctor:
Internal characteristics (fractures of bones, deviances of organs . . .)
Outward characteristics (birthmarks, color of the eyes, the hair, height, weight, body structure, physical deformations, joint picture of the victim . . .)
Where do these utterly characteristics appear:
Very detailed character description done by the family:
Very detailed character description by classmates, teachers etc. . . .:
Hobbies:
Sport:
Friends:
Clothes at the time of the disappearance:
Dental records:
Glasses:
Tattoos:
Place of tattoos:
Does the victim speak different languages:

3. Family circumstances

One parent family:
Lives with father:
Lives with mother:
Others:
Conflict situations:
Institutions:
Homes:
Foster parents:
Work address – father:
Work address – mother:
Are there any family members with a criminal record:
Are there any neighbours or friends with a criminal record:
Who:
Why:
Names of friends of the family:
Descriptions of neighbors:
Are there people known in the area for child sex offences:
Name:
Address:
Where are these people at the moment:
Have they been seen in the vicinity of the child lately:

4. Eventual supplementary information:

In case of child murder.

Same as above but the circumstances of the discovery of the body has to be noted in detail:

5. Data and parameters

Time, day, month, year of discovery:
Body found by:
Did the finder touch anything at the crime scene or the body:
What was it:
Where has the victim been found (city, village, . . .)
(Detailed pictures of the crime scene have to be added to the file)
Area (wood, station, centre of the city, parking area . . .)
(Detailed pictures of the whole area have to be added)
Meteorological circumstances at the time of discovery:
Are there witnesses that saw the victim in that area:
Who:
Time (sure or not sure):
Accompanied by who (give description):
Was a vehicle seen:
Description of vehicle:
Death causes:
Date, hour of death:
Stomach content (detailed):
(Join pictures of autopsy:
Are there clothes missing:
Which ones:
In what circumstances have the clothes of the victim been found:
Are there jewels missing:
Which:
Are there other things missing from the victim:
Which ones:
Are there objects on the crime scene that do not belong there:
Which ones:
Is there something specific that strikes you as odd:

Describe:
How has the victim been found:
In what position:
How could the victim have been transported to that spot (car, train, on foot . . .)
Was the victim raped:
Is DNA material found:
Are there other signs of violence on the victim:
Did the victim defend itself:
Is DNA found in the eventual wounds of the victim:
Examine the crime scene well before touching anything, note every detail and your remarks. Is there evidence that could fit a certain signature of the criminal:
Describe your own finding in detail:
Is there evidence of over killing?
Comments:
Is there evidence of bite marks on the victim:
Evidence that could show torture:
Has a weapon been used:
Which one:
Are there ropes or other binding materials used to restrain and control the victim:
Could these objects have been brought to the crime scene by the offender or was it possibly that he found it at the crime scene itself:
Is the place of the discovery of the body the same as the place of the murder:
Is the victim found near her/his home:
Distance:
Is it possible that the victim met her offender at the crime scene:
Who could possibly be a witness of the crime:
Name:
Address:
Is there evidence of a great deal of violence:
Describe:
Is there evidence of a fire at or in the surroundings of the crime scene:
Is there evidence of dead animals at or in the surrounding of the crime scene:
Is there evidence of ritual acts at or in the surroundings of the crime scene?

Is there evidence of human feces at or in the surroundings of the crime scene:
Was the victim visible at the crime scene:
Was it covered:
With what:
Had body parts been removed from the victim:
Which ones:
How:
Is semen found in the victim's mouth:
Was the victim blindfolded when found:
Is there evidence that she/he was blindfolded before:
Was the face of the victim covered:
Was the face turned to the ground:
Is there evidence that the victim has been dressed after death by the criminal:
Make a list of all holiday visits of the victim:
Supplementary information:

This is initial information about the victim. It is evident that this list can be extended. We will now look at the information we can gather about the criminal. Sometimes we have a suspect who is not known but about whom the police can have very clear suspicions about his part in the act.

6. Status of the criminal

Name:
Family name:
Address:
Age:
Place of birth:
Other addresses in the present and the past:
Sex:
Race:
Height, weight, body construction:
Colour of the hair and hair style:
Glasses:
Beard, moustache, other marks:

Cicatrices, birthmarks:
Tattoos (describe):
Area of the tattoos:
Are there visible marks of importance (limping, tics, paralyses . . .):
Earlier condemnations:
Which ones:
When:
Prison sentences:
When did he leave prison:
Mental hospital:
Relation to the victim:
Military service:
Vehicle:
Driver's license:
Does the suspect know the area where the victim has been found:
Does the suspect know the area where the victim disappeared:
Does the suspect know the area where the victim lived:
Does the suspect know other members of the family or friends of the family:
Where did the suspect spend his holidays:
Is the suspect socially adapted:

All these elements need to be introduced in a central database that gathers and analyzes information from all over the world. Thanks to this central management we will be able to make links between the different crimes. It is a way to arrest criminals who otherwise can continue for many years with their destructive work, faster. Sometimes we find the body of a little child in one country and do not know who this child is. It happens that a body is found in Germany that in fact comes from Spain. Recently an American has been arrested in Miami for the murder of a thirteen year old girl in France. The American was originally from Spain.

As long as we have no central database to join all the information, we will not be able to link crimes together and criminals know that. It is evident that such a project fails or succeeds with the good cooperation of different police departments all over the world. It must be excluded that politicians get involved in this.

II. A prison for child killers.

Although there is little chance that such a model will ever be taken into consideration, I will try to draw such a model. It is a structure that was taken seriously in the United States as well as in France. It is a base concept that can be adapted based on suggestions and ideas.

For a population of fifteen child killers, we need approximately twenty specialized people for supervision, study work and therapy: four psychologists specialized in child sex offences and one psychiatrist also specially formed for this work, a doctor, a director of the prison, two assistants, three guards, a cleaning team of two people, a chef, a lawyer, three experienced policemen and eventually two investigators or research judges.

The following subjects need to be considered:

a) Group therapy
b) re-education programmes and activities
c) a research team
d) a drama team
e) individual therapy
f) relaxation therapy
g) anger management
h) the cooperation of the prisoners in working on cold cases of child disappearances and child murder
i) external services who need to be consulted by the client when he is released after his sentence
j) reintegration in society
k) a lifetime follow up of the client

Weekly program of the prison:

Monday:

10.00-11.00   Group therapy (group I)

11.00-11.30	pause
11.30-13.00	group therapy or individual therapy
13.00-14.00	lunch
14.00-15.00	discussion with the group on the progress of the week
15.00-15.30	pause
15.30-16.30	evaluation of the past week
16.30-17.30	study an unsolved case in group or individual under the supervision of therapist or a policeman

Tuesday:

10.00-11.00	group therapy (group II)
11.00-11.30	coffee/tea
11.30-13.00	individual evaluation or group evaluation
13.00-14.00	lunch
14.00-16.00	working on an unsolved case with group II
16.00-18.00	evaluation with the team

Wednesday:

10.00-11.00	group therapy (group I)
11.00-11.30	coffee/tea
11.30-13.00	evaluation in group or individual (group II)
13.00-14.00	lunch
14.00-16.00	assertivity training (group II)
16.00-17.30	drama (theatre and role play)

Thursday:

10.00-11.00	re-education
11.00-11.30	coffee/tea
11.30-13.00	meeting with group I and group II
13.00-14.00	lunch
14.00-15.00	group therapy of individual therapy
15.00-16.00	relaxation therapy

Friday:

10.00-11.00	Sports
11.00-11.30	coffee/tea
11.30-13.00	evaluation with all prisoners
13.00-14.00	lunch

The afternoon is spent on sports activities, relaxation, individual work, painting, drawing, reading ...

1. We can work around one specific sexual crime as well as individual or group
2. It is the therapist who decides if an activity will take place in group or individually
3. A group is coached by two professionals, but days are foreseen where a criminal himself can lead a group under the supervision of a professional.

During all sessions the client has to take notes of everything done during the week. He has to show them to his personal therapist. He is allowed to make his own remarks and propositions.

To make a diversity of different types of child killers in such a closed system, we take criminals of each type of child killers:

> One impulsive type of criminal
> One methodical type of criminal
> One mixed type (methodical/impulsive)
> One methodical/psychopathic type
> One impulsive/psychopathic type
> One methodical/homosexual type
> One impulsive/homosexual type
> One impulsive/sadistic type
> One narcistic perverse type.

III. Degree of dangerosity of a criminal – Inventory and Evaluation

In the first instance this inventory tries to study and characterize the violent reactions of the individual. This phenomological enterprise (study by observation) as a goal to gain an objective insight in the way the individual reacts. The fundamental purpose is that we have to verify the dangers linked to this. Consultations with clinical therapists show that it is very difficult to have such a clear insight into the violent behavior of clients. It is indispensable to invest time for this aspect of the evaluation that often because of emotional reasons is put aside. The consequences of this are that we risk to underestimate or overestimate the violence of the client. This information has to be added to other objective conclusions and then divided into four main themes.

The first theme contains the elements linked to the identification of the violent phenomena. It is important to make a distinction between the violent behavior, the threats and the violent fantasies. One must be able to estimate as precise as possible the real impact of the violent phenomena. On the one side there is the quantitative aspect (the degree of violent behavior) whereas we also try to measure the frequency of this violent behavior. On the other side we have to consider the qualitative aspect. This helps us to identify if the violence is directed towards objects or persons, and if a weapon is used which kind of weapon is it?

The second theme concerns the victim. We need to identify the victim to be able to understand the relation between victim and criminal. Moreover it is important to investigate which specific characteristics the victim has. Also the way in which victim and offender meet each other (at the time of the crime) is important to identify.

The third theme gathers the information about the crime scene.

In the fourth theme a report is made that identifies the degree of importance of the time between violent fantasies and realization in reality. This information gives us an idea of the mental functioning of the client and the evolution of his violent impulses.

Factors that are linked with the violent acting out.

The systematic violent acting out has lead to an investigation. An analysis is made about the degree of dangerosity of this violent act. Therewith the factors are examined that can be linked to the act. These factors are categorized in five parts: static factors, dynamic factors, situational factors, biological factors and factors that are linked to the mental health of the individual.

1. The static factors:

The static factors gather the information about the identity of the criminal; for instance: his psychiatric files, the medical-legal file, the eventual surgery the criminal underwent during his life and the juridical aspects of his life. Experts in the field point out the importance of these factors. We have to consider them as unchangeable for the criminal. They are part of his past and his hereby built character. When we examine each of those factors separately, they seem unimportant. We cannot change them and it is difficult to know what the actual impact is on their life. But when we put those static factors together with other factors of the violent behavior, we can see that indeed they play an important role in the chain of the violence that results in the committing of the crime.

2. The dynamic factors:

Although these elements are very useful in the understanding of the crime, we see that they are often neglected. Intra-psychic conflicts are often the basis of an important amount of violent crimes. Some conflicts (dynamic factors) will be the engine of the violent behavior against another individual, depending on the psychopathological type. The triggers that provoke violent behavior are: fear to fall apart, fear for divorce or rejection and symbiotic fear. These fears are linked to a sexually disturbed identity of the individual or his feeling of narcistic vulnerability. As well the paranoïc schizofrenic client who lives in a symbiotic relationship with his mother, as the narcistic client who idealizes his female partner, can react extremely on the unforeseen separation of them. The knowledge of the deeper and hidden dynamical factors is thus essential if we want to prepare such a person to eventual painful separations in his life.

Symbolic objects also seem to be important in the psycho-dynamic sense. They help understand the violent act. It is therefore also important to understand and examine the defense mechanisms which go with the violence or which precede the violence. The denial, the projection-identification system, the gap between criminal and society and the idealisation of the mother or the partner are often determining factors with violent offenders. Often they go hand in hand with the complete absence of empathy and a lack of psychic processing of a problem.

3. The situational factors:

In antagonism with other factors the situational factors or surroundings factors are generally well assessed. But they are underestimated. The clinical material is spontaneously offered by the client to the therapist, who only gives little attention to this material. Unfortunately this information gets lost in the amount of information gathered about a crime. The situational factors have everything to do with biological, psychological and social stress elements that precede the weeks before the actual crime. These stressful elements get the value the individual wants to give to them, depending on his own vulnerability. Special attention has to be given to the separation of loved ones in the past of the criminal.

4. The biological factors:

When certain biological deviancies (which are not always the case) are found with a client with violent behavior, they are in general minimized, hidden or explained based on the psychopathological state of the client. The therapist interprets certain hidden or even visible clinical signs as a brain deviation. With non-violent clients we not always take the same steps as with the violent ones. A deeper knowledge of the biological deviancies makes it though possible to work out a treatment plan that is adapted to the client. Such a treatment plan is more limited and more realistic. The pharmacological strategies can also better be applied.

A profound evaluation has to be made of the intellectual functioning of the client. The clear limits in this evaluation area create irritation with the therapist because he often overestimates the intelligence quotient of his or her client. Manipulation is not the same as intelligence. And many violent clients are good manipulators. This doesn't mean that they are very intelligent. We also sometimes see that the reluctance and poor cooperation of the client is wrongly judged and seen as a resistance to cooperate, while in fact we are confronted with someone who can not deal with a certain level of therapy.

A systematical clinical examination helps us to identify the sources of factors linked to the mental state of mind of the client. We have to ask direct and precise questions to know what his ideas are about violence. Many clients are unable to express verbally painful emotions and fears they daily feel. They are unable to describe them. We can compare it to people who have the intention to commit suicide but who decline this idea when they are able to talk about their despair and deathly desires.

The gathering of information about the degree of dangerosity of the client has to be done in a structured way and in a safe context. But the therapist has to feel safe too. On the one hand the therapist get information that makes a clear image of the degree of dangerosity of the client and on the other hand he or she gains insight into important elements that trigger the reactions to violent acting out. The therapist will soon be able to evaluate and re-evaluate the diagnostic of each client separately.

5. The level of recognition.

The degree in which the client recognizes his amount of violence of his crime is linked to defense mechanisms he uses. This recognition level can also be linked to diverse biological factors which disturb or limit the brain function. Hereby the client can become very upset and confused in his thinking.

Does the client realize that he is on the point of committing a violent crime?

Can he recognize the signals that preceded the crime?

Did he have other alternative strategies to avoid a violent crime?

If he is able to answer these questions, he gives precious information about the possibility of building up a good therapeutic bond.

IV. Childhood of murderers – talking figures.

In the United States professionals did very deep research to the childhood of murderers of all kind. The figures of the FBI in Washington D.C. of 1995 show us the next information:

35 % of the killers witnessed sexual violence in their childhood
35 % witnessed abnormal sex (sex with animals, objects, bondage, SM . . .) of their parents
42 % witnessed abnormal sex by strangers
43 % was sexually abused as a child
71 % was a voyeur as a child (peeping while others have sex)
73 % was exposed to stress situations linked with sex
81 % was exposed to pornography

74 % of the killers were psychological abused in the family. The term 'psychological abuse' covers a whole area. When we consider the story of John in this book, we can see that he has been used throughout his whole life for all kind of purposes. A child prevented from growing up to an adolescent or an adult is also a form of psychological abuse. Never taking the feelings or the wishes of a child or never being rewarded but only punished a child can have severe psychological consequences. Parents that constantly correct their children, are never are there when their children need them, that make no time to listen to them, that never participate in school events while other parents are present, that too is child abuse. Many children complain that their parents constantly argue and that they the children are often the target. In some cases parents or caretakers never say anything nice to their children. 'You are nothing, you are stupid, you are too slow, too lazy, and you cannot do anything right, you are always late, you're ugly, you're fat, and your teeth are crooked . . .' With such messages no child can develop a steady self image and it is evident that it will be decisive to make its view on the world. But also parents who over-indulge their children and are over-protective are abusive.

The FBI collected more figures. They are a revelation in the context of the childhood of later killers. I made a choice in these figures. I suppose the figures speak for themselves:

Behavior of (later) murderers:

	Childhood	Adolescence	Adulthood
Daydreaming	82 %	81 %	81 %
Compulsive Masturbation	82 %	82 %	81 %
Loneliness/Isolation	71 %	77 %	73 %
Chronic lying	71 %	75 %	68 %
Bedwetting	68 %	60 %	15 %
Tantrums	67 %	84 %	72 %
Nightmares	67 %	68 %	52 %
Vandalism	58 %	62 %	35 %
Pyromania	56 %	52 %	28 %
Kleptomania	56 %	56 %	81 %
Cruelty towards younger children	54 %	64 %	44 %
Low self esteem	52 %	63 %	62 %
Sleeping problems	48 %	50 %	50 %
Violence towards adults	38 %	84 %	86 %
Phobias	38 %	43 %	50 %

Running away from home	36 %	46 %	11 %
Cruelty towards animals	36 %	46 %	36 %
Headaches	29 %	33 %	45 %
Eating impairment	27 %	36 %	35 %
Convulsions	19 %	21 %	13 %
Self mutilation	19 %	21 %	32 %

The percentages seem to decrease with age. It is possible that it means that adults found ways to canalize their frustrations and problems. But a great deal of them finds ways to criminality.

The chronic lying can have several sources. Some children try to protect their fictitious world of fantasies against intruders, with lies. When people ask them: "why did you do that?" the child will not want to answer: "Because I dreamt of doing this since so long . . ."
No, it will invent a lie. For some children lying is a way to attract attention.

But an overview of the above figures makes it clear that children are fragile and vulnerable and we have to protect them. It is up to us adults to say NO to abuse. It is up to us adults to start prevention campaigns to warn abusive adults that they are watched and that they and not their children are responsible for abusive behavior.

Because indeed:

A world of wanted children would make a world of difference.

Made in the USA
Monee, IL
04 February 2023